Kitchen Party

EFFORTLESS RECIPES FOR EVERY OCCASION

Mary Berg

appetite
by RANDOM HOUSE

Library and Archives of Canada Cataloguing in Publication is available upon request.

ISBN: 9780147531247
eBook ISBN: 9780147531254

Cover and book design by Jennifer Griffiths
Photography by Lauren Vandenbrook

Printed and bound in China

Published in Canada by Appetite by Random House™, a division of Penguin Random House LLC.

www.penguinrandomhouse.ca

10 9 8 7 6 5 4 3

appetite by RANDOM HOUSE | Penguin Random House Canada

"When you love what you do and you respect the ingredients, food becomes magic. That's exactly what Mary has done in her first cookbook and that's also why she holds the title of Canada's MasterChef!"
Chef Claudio Aprile

EVERYONE KNOWS THAT A GOOD PARTY ends up in the kitchen, whether you're grabbing a drink, tasting a dish, or just chatting with the host and other guests. That's because the kitchen is the heart of every home, big or small. But sometimes entertaining (even casually) can feel daunting or overwhelming, with all the planning, shopping, cooking, and clean up. Enter Mary Berg . . .

In her first book, TV star and home cook Mary Berg is here to banish any anxiety about preparing food for the people you love. All of Mary's recipes are meant to be laid down on a table that is groaning under the weight of delicious food and relaxed elbows. *Kitchen Party* is filled with Mary's family-style favorites for brunches, dinners, and special occasions—along with some of her famous baked goods and desserts, of course. You'll find over 100 simple, straightforward and mouthwateringly-good recipes for dishes like Blueberry Cheesecake French Toast Bake with Apple Cinnamon Syrup; Ricotta, Roasted Grapes and Hazelnut Tartines; Flank Steak with Horseradish Cream; and Slablova (aka Pavlova for a Crowd). And with Mary's tips and suggested menu pairings for multiple occasions, from Mother's Day Brunch to a Low-Key Bridal Shower, you'll never find yourself short of ideas.

Whether you're cooking for a big crowd of friends or hosting a romantic dinner for two, Mary is here to guide you using the warmth and cooking skills that have already made her a beloved voice of encouragement for all types of home cooks.

For Aaron and Myra,
my forever party guests

Contents

Brunch Parties

FOR THE EARLY BIRDS AMONG US

Cocktail Parties

FOR AN INDECISIVE HOST

Dinner Parties

FOR LEISURELY DINERS

Special Occasion Menus

FOR INDULGENT TIMES

Party of Two

FOR THE ROMANTICS* IN THE CROWD

** Meals can easily be shared between non-romantically-involved pairs*

Introduction

"One cannot think well, love well, sleep well, if one has not dined well."

Virginia Woolf

"This much I knew: If you are what you eat, then I only want to eat the good stuff."

Remy, *Ratatouille*

I love food. That's probably the most basic and universally agreed-upon statement you've ever heard, right? But as clichéd as it might sound, it's true! I love everything about food—from planning and shopping, to cooking and eating. I love how food has the ability to bring people together, to transport a person from the stresses of their day, and to convey so much love in just a few bites.

The classic kindergarten mantra of "sharing is caring" is something I continue to live by, especially when it comes to food. Cooking, baking, and eating are some of the most social acts that I take part in every day, and I suspect the same might be true for you. Everyone has had days where the only thing that has pulled them out of a slump was baking and eating a whole batch of chocolate chip cookies but, most of the time, we cook for others. My husband, Aaron, often quips that when I'm left to cook only for myself, I eat like a raccoon, grabbing handfuls of pretzels, raw carrot sticks, and spoonfuls of whatever leftovers are hanging around the fridge. For me, half the fun of food is in preparing it for others, so why would I bother whipping up an exciting meal if I'm left to eat it all on my lonesome? In my house, any excuse I can think of is reason enough to invite friends over to share in a meal, grand or humble. Whenever I have people over, the festivities always revolve around the kitchen. No matter the occasion, during at least one point, every single person in attendance will be packed into my tiny scullery, chitchatting away, tasting things here and there, and dipping into the fridge for another drink. This is what I call a kitchen party.

For many Canadians, the term "kitchen party" is evocative of the East Coast. Renowned for their hospitality, good home cooking, and great music, East Coasters are arguably the chief experts in bringing friends and family together for informal parties centered on the heart of the home. In my family, this tradition has evolved from our East Coast roots but really, gathering around the comfort of a hearth of any description is something everyone can relate to. Kitchen parties should be overflowing with great company and good food—food that people want to eat, that might remind them of an old favorite. It should be the type of food that invites you to get your hands dirty, help yourself to a few more forkfuls, and nosh away for hours, surrounded by friends and family.

Kitchen Party: Cooking for Those You Love is here to banish any inflated pomp, circumstance, and anxiety surrounding the idea of inviting people into your home. This is a cookbook to complement parties that last for hours, allowing you to really catch up in the complete comfort of your own home. It's filled to the brim with family-style dishes for brunches, cocktails, dinners, and special occasions—along with some baked goods and desserts, of course. They're clear, simple, and straightforward recipes that are grand enough for company, yet easy enough to accomplish on a regular Tuesday night. They're meant to be plunked down on a table that is groaning under the weight of delicious food and relaxed elbows. Each and every morsel has been put through the rigorous Myra Berg litmus test, meaning that if my wonderful and kitchen-inept mother can make it, anyone can! So go ahead—fill this book with sticky notes, dog-ear the pages, mark it up with pens and some kitchen mess, and try halving your favorite recipes if you're cooking for smaller numbers.

From my kitchen to yours, *Kitchen Party* is here to make you look like the culinary wizard I know you are and to help you experience the same joy that I do when I'm cooking for and sharing food with those I love.

Welcome to the party!

Mary xo ox

Mary

Cook's Notes

I've always loved this section in cookbooks. It makes me feel like a fly on the wall, figuring out what little things help make someone's pantry so perfect, fridge so fabulous, and eats so enticing.

In my kitchen, all pepper is freshly ground or cracked, and I always have a few types of salt on hand. I find traditional table salt to be quite harsh, and it tends to trigger flashbacks of childhood sore throat remedies, so kosher is my salt of choice, with fine sea salt coming into play every once in a while. Lemon and lime juice are always freshly squeezed, whereas orange juice can be interchanged with store-bought unless otherwise stated in a recipe.

All dairy, including cheese, sour cream, and yogurt, is full-fat, as that is what works best in both baking and cooking (and is just what I prefer to snack on). For milk, all recipes have been tested with whole, but you can use 2% in a pinch. When a recipe calls for cream, the fat percentage will be specified.

For any baked goods, ingredients like milk, butter, cream cheese, and eggs should be at room temperature for best results unless the recipe tells you otherwise.

For those of you who don't know me, I don't eat poultry, beef, or pork, but as a good deal of my love for cooking stems from my love of sharing with friends and family, I prepare meat relatively regularly. When meat is on the menu, I always try to buy what I call "happy meat" from a reputable source, one where I know the animals have been well treated.

The same goes for seafood. Overfishing continues to be an issue for our oceans and lakes, so please consider checking out the lists of sustainable seafood choices provided by Ocean Wise, the Marine Stewardship Council, and the Monterey Bay Aquarium Seafood Watch:

oceanwise.ca/sustainable-seafood
msc.org
seafoodwatch.org

When developing these recipes, I made sure to use ingredients that can be easily found in an average grocery store (save for a couple of special mix-ins or cocktail garnishes that can be found at specialty

shops or online). I also tested all of the recipes with standard kitchen tools and equipment. I'm not going to ask you to use a kitchen unitasker, because that's just not the way I cook. If a job can be done with a vegetable peeler, it'll be done with a vegetable peeler.

In terms of recipe prep and general organization, I would be lost without my arsenal of reusable storage containers, plastic wrap, aluminum foil, sticky notes, and a permanent marker or two. This helps me get all of my prep work out of the way before I even start cooking so that I won't be bothered with any finicky kitchen tasks as something threatens to bubble over on the stove or after my guests arrive.

Last-minute tastes while you cook are a must in order to see what your dish needs to really make it sing. Does it taste dull? Add a squidge of lemon. A little flat? Some kosher salt will perk it right up. Is there something missing but you just can't put your finger on what it is? Give a knob of butter a try. Even if it doesn't help, butter is amazing, so it's obviously not a *bad* idea. These might sound like silly steps, but that last hit of something can help awaken your taste buds and take a dish from good to great.

Finally, the best tip I can offer is that, in the kitchen, there are only varying degrees of success. That means that success could take the

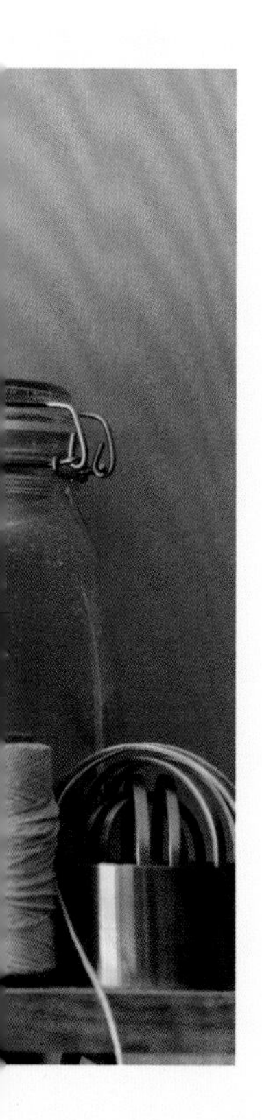

form of discovering how to burn something to a blackened crisp—so now I know how long *not* to cook it for. Success is a state of mind. Approach every meal you cook and every party you host with this at the back of your mind and you'll be a culinary maven in no time.

For now, please come have a look in my pantry, fridge, and drawers and see some of the sometimes-overlooked must-haves in my kitchen:

Food:

All-purpose flour
Canned crushed tomatoes
Cooking onions
Cornmeal
Dark or light brown sugar, can be used interchangeably
Dried herb blend such as herbes du Provence or Italian seasoning
Extra virgin olive oil
Fine sea salt
Fresh herbs
Full-fat mayonnaise
Good-quality balsamic vinegar
Granulated sugar
Instant (rapid-rise) and active dry (traditional) yeast
Instant espresso powder
Kosher salt
Large eggs
Lemons
Limes
Neutral oil such as vegetable, grapeseed, or canola
No- or low-sodium chicken, vegetable, and beef broth
Olive oil
Three or four types of hard and/or soft cheese
Unsalted butter
Vegetable oil
White, red wine, and cider vinegar
Whole wheat flour

Things:

A 1 oz and 2 oz spring-loaded ice cream scoop
Baking sheets (with rims)
Balloon whisk
Blender
Candy thermometer
Digital probe thermometer
Enameled Dutch oven
Fine rasp or microplane
Frying pan
Full-sized food processor
Heatproof spatula
Knives—one or two really good ones
Large wooden cutting board
Notebooks or a clipboard
Pens and pencils
Plastic wrap, parchment paper, and aluminum foil
Reusable containers
Serving dishes and spoons
Spring-loaded tongs
Stand mixer
Well-seasoned cast iron skillet
Wire roasting/cooling racks

Preparing for a Party

When it comes to throwing a kitchen party, I live by one main rule: An organized host is a relaxed host and a relaxed host makes a good party.

In this book, I am not going to tell you what music to put on your playlist or whether or not you need to put out place cards. Personally, I think that's a little over the top for a kitchen party, but if it's your style, go for it. At its core, *Kitchen Party* is about enjoying food with friends and family with as much or as little pomp and circumstance as you want—it's whatever works best for you.

Now, I realize that my love of cooking can sometimes blind me to the fact that, all things considered, getting food on the table any day—let alone when you're having guests over—is a lot of work. There's planning, shopping, and prep, all before the oven gets turned on—and don't even get me started with cleanup! I often overlook these things because cooking has always been the most satisfying and relaxing part of my day, but I know that that is not the case for everyone. In order to help you prepare for your kitchen party, I've created these recipes with your schedule and other daily commitments in mind. I've written them in the most straightforward way possible and I'd never dream of giving you unnecessary steps. Some recipe methods might seem a little long, but that's because they are filled to the brim with tips and tricks to help set you on the right path toward the most beautiful and delicious results. I've also taken the liberty of noting any "make-ahead" tips, kitchen hacks, or shortcuts that will help you prepare these recipes easily and quickly, making you look like the most amazing chef/host ever.

In addition to the tips in the recipes themselves, there are a few that I use regularly to help keep me on track and stay cool and collected in the kitchen, whether I'm making dinner for just Aaron and me or preparing a massive holiday feast.

My first step toward kitchen party success is planning a menu. Flip through this book and take note of any recipes you think you'd like to try or, if you're looking for some extra inspiration, take a look at Menus from My Kitchen on page 244. Consider the number of people you will be feeding and think about appetites. Do you need a main and three sides, or would a main, one side, and a few snacky cocktail apps work? In my experience, people often overestimate how much food and

variety they actually need. If I'm having a larger number of guests over for cocktails, that doesn't necessarily mean that I have to whip up twice as many recipes; instead I will often just divide recipes between two serving dishes. This diminishes the chances of your guests involuntarily finding themselves in an awkward mini sword fight over a single cheeseboard. For a larger dinner party, if you're whipping up a hearty main like Red Wine–Braised English-Cut Short Ribs (page 128) with Blue Cheese Polenta (page 132), some easy make-ahead snacks like Marinated Olives (page 76) or Roasted Tomatoes (page 79) would be perfect as apps. Grazing snacks like these are a host's best friend, as they tend to keep your guests occupied while you do any last- minute prep in the kitchen.

While you're planning your menu and reading through the recipes, take note of any potential shortcuts, whether that means partially or fully prepping some items ahead of time or using some store-bought items to make your job easier. For instance, if you know you'll be crunched for time but want to make No-Knead Bread and Homemade

Sugar
Lemons

Butter (page 102), consider buying a good loaf of crusty bread from your local bakery and whipping up the butter yourself. Your guests will love it just as much.

As you read through your selected recipes, make sure that they work together, not just in terms of flavor but also within the confines of your kitchen. Ask yourself questions like:

- Is there enough room in my oven or on the stove for these recipes?
- Does the oven temperature for the main dish work with the sides?
- How much can I prepare in advance?
- How much time will I need to spend in the kitchen once people start arriving?

I always try to do a quick run-through of the evening in my head, considering that I too want to enjoy the party! When you plan a meal that you can accomplish without having a meltdown in the kitchen, whether it's made up of one dish or six, each and every guest will be impressed.

The next step is what I like to call the "list phase." It is just as dorky and Type A as it sounds, but it is so helpful. I'm kind of crazy when it comes to making lists, but I think they are so important when it comes to success in the kitchen. The first list I like to make is just a simple rundown of the ingredients needed to make a recipe. After doing that, I "shop" my pantry and fridge to figure out what I already have and narrow down what I need to pick up at the grocery store. After crossing off everything I have in stock, I organize the remaining ingredients according to how I walk around my local grocery store. This might seem like a silly step, but when I write out my second list, my shopping list (starting with produce, moving on to the deli and bakery counters, meat and fish sections, the middle aisles, and, finally, frozen items and dairy products), I never have to ping-pong my way through a grocery store and I know for certain that I have everything I need to pull off a recipe.

The final list I like to make is more of a play-by-play for my kitchen party. This list is essentially a detailed but rough schedule for the day and is typically affixed to a tattered old clipboard—my most trusted tool in the kitchen when I'm having guests over. The day before a party of any caliber, whether it's a Christmas feast or a casual Friday night get-together, I sit down with my recipes and plan out what I need to do and when, with a careful eye toward anything and everything that can be prepared ahead. This list helps me wrap my head around the flow of

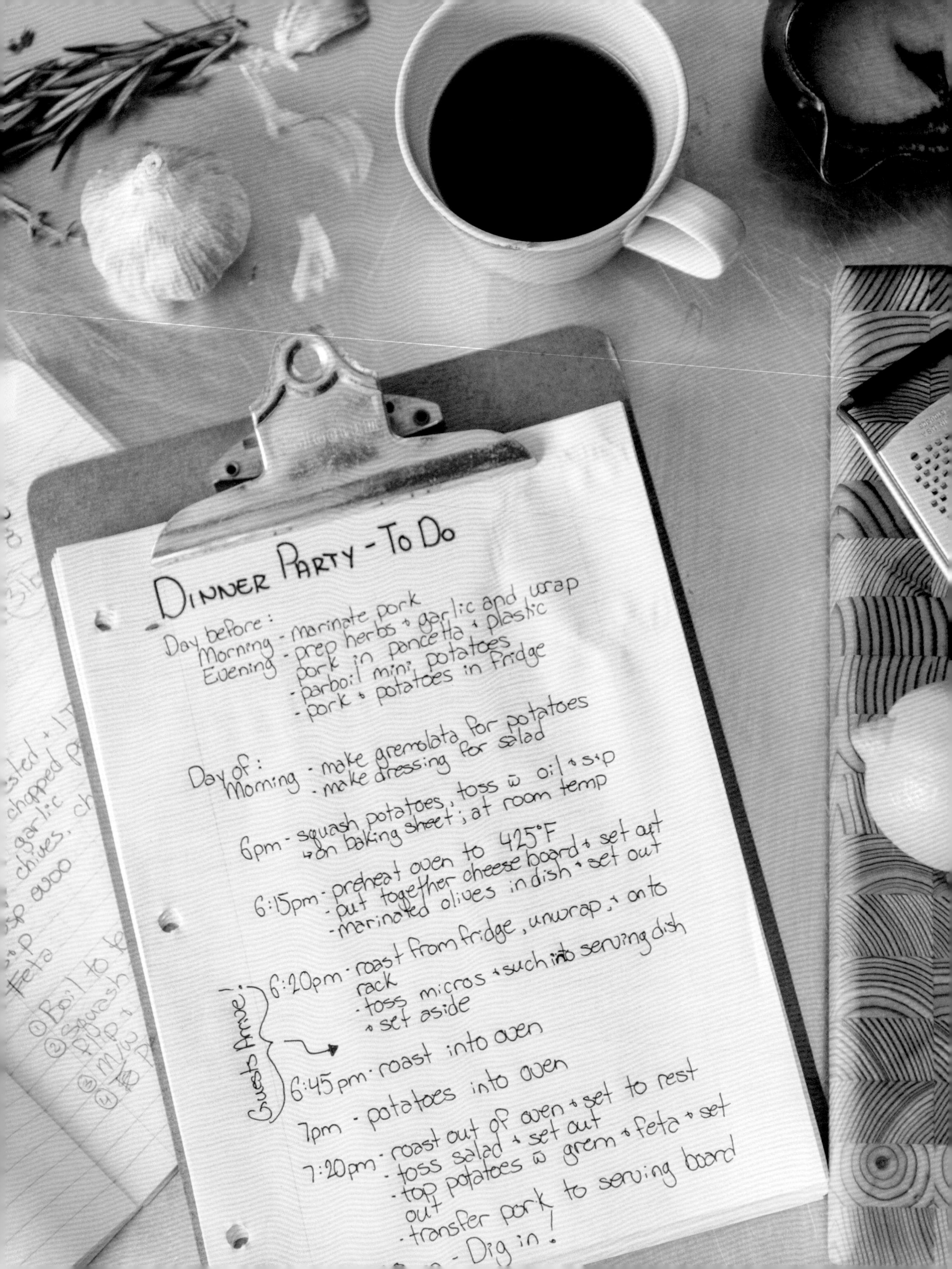

Dinner Party - To Do

Day before:
Morning - marinate pork
Evening - prep herbs + garlic and wrap pork in pancetta + plastic
- parboil mini potatoes
- pork + potatoes in fridge

Day of:
Morning - make gremolata for potatoes
- make dressing for salad

6pm - squash potatoes, toss w oil + s+p + on baking sheet; at room temp

6:15pm - preheat oven to 425°F
- put together cheese board + set out
- marinated olives in dish + set out

6:20pm - roast from fridge, unwrap, + onto rack
- toss micros + such into serving dish
+ set aside

Guests Arrive! → roast into oven

6:45pm - potatoes into oven

7pm - roast out of oven + set to rest

7:20pm - toss salad + set out
- top potatoes w grem + feta + set out
- transfer pork to serving board
- Dig in!

the evening, keeps me on track, and lets me know that I'm not forgetting any details in the excitement of a party.

To make this list, I start with the time I would like everything to be done, plated, and served. Dessert doesn't usually make it onto the list, as it is almost always prepared far in advance and is served whenever full stomachs will allow. From there, I work backward, breaking each recipe down into small steps, from prep to cooking, and finally serving. For example, if I'm making Pancetta Pork Tenderloin (page 122) as my main dish, the recipe tells me that I need to marinate the pork for up to 24 hours and that I can prepare the roast the night before. The prepared tenderloin needs to come out of the fridge to come to room temperature for 20 minutes and then go into the oven for 30 to 35 minutes, followed by 10 minutes' resting. If I'm planning on serving dinner at 7:30, I know that I can have the pork tenderloins marinated and wrapped the night before, so that on the day of the party, all I need to do is take the pork out of the fridge at 6:20 and have it in the oven at 6:45. If I'm serving Squashed Potatoes with Gremolata and Feta (page 136) and an Herb Salad with My Go-To Dressing (page 228) as sides, I do the same thing with those recipes and slot them into the schedule accordingly, again making sure to take advantage of anything I can do ahead. Basically, this leaves me with little more to do than pop potatoes and pork into the oven, give the salad a toss, and place all of the dishes on their serving platters to head to the table after my guests have arrived.

Learning about timing your recipes can sometimes sound intimidating, but I promise, it's not as complicated as it might seem. Take a deep breath. You can do this! With a little organization, no matter what's on the menu, all you'll need to do is go into the kitchen once or twice to pull something from the oven, give a dish a final season or stir, and serve your beautiful masterpieces to friends and family. After all, food and drinks are great, but really, kitchen parties are all about bringing together the people you love.

Brunch Parties

FOR THE EARLY BIRDS AMONG US

Green Tea Sangria

SERVES 8–10

- 2 cups ice
- 2 cups chilled unsweetened green tea, store-bought or home-brewed
- ½ cup gin
- ½ cup elderflower liqueur
- ¼ cup lime juice (about 2 limes)
- ½ cup fresh mint leaves, roughly torn
- ½ cup fresh basil leaves, roughly torn
- ¼ cucumber, thinly sliced
- 1 lime, thinly sliced
- 1 bottle dry sparkling wine

I like to convince myself that this sangria is more of a health drink than anything else. You've got juice, fruit, and, in this case, the revitalizing powers of green tea. If you ignore the gin, liqueur, and bubbly, it's practically something you'd drink after six hours of yoga at a spa, right?

In a large pitcher filled with the ice, stir together the chilled green tea, gin, elderflower liqueur, lime juice, mint leaves, basil leaves, cucumber, and lime. Add in the sparkling wine and serve straight away.

If you'd like to make this sangria ahead of time, just omit the ice and bubbly until serving time and store it in the fridge so that the flavors can get to know each other a little.

Note:
I like to use cava or prosecco in this sangria, but if you're not into bubbly, feel free to swap it out with a crisp bottle of sauvignon blanc.

Iced Dirty Chai Latte

SERVES 6–8

- 1 tablespoon green cardamom pods
- 4 cinnamon sticks
- 3 allspice berries
- 1 teaspoon whole cloves
- ⅛ teaspoon whole black peppercorns
- 1 (2-inch) piece fresh ginger, peeled and sliced
- 1 vanilla bean, split in half
- 6 tablespoons brown sugar
- 6 black tea bags
- 4 cups milk
- 1–1½ cups strong coffee or espresso
- Ice cubes

On a recent trip down to the Bay Area in California, I discovered a few things. The first is that San Francisco is great but also disorienting, and I much prefer places a little away from the main drag, like nearby Larkspur and Muir Woods. The second is that Trader Joe's is exactly what I wanted it to be—their pastrami-cured smoked salmon is the bee's knees. The third and final thing is the glory that is a Dirty Chai Latte. A little café around the corner from our place in Larkspur introduced me to this gem that is essentially just a chai latte with a shot of espresso added for good measure. Apparently, it's a pretty normal order for those in the know, so for those of you who, like me, are less than savvy when it comes to swanky coffee, welcome to the know!

Set a small frying pan over medium-high heat. Using the side of a large knife, gently press down on the cardamom pods to crack them open. Transfer the pods and any loose seeds to the pan along with the cinnamon sticks, allspice berries, cloves, and peppercorns. Toast the spices, stirring often, until slightly fragrant, about 3 minutes.

Transfer the toasted spices to a medium pot set over medium-high heat and add in the ginger and vanilla bean, and then the brown sugar, along with 4 cups of water. Bring the mixture to a boil, turn down the heat to low, cover the pot, and let it all simmer for 20 minutes. Remove the pot from the heat and add in the tea bags. Allow the tea to steep, uncovered, for 5 minutes. Pour this chai syrup through a fine mesh sieve into a large heat-resistant pitcher, add in the milk, and chill in the fridge until very cold.

To serve, fill your glasses about halfway with ice. Pour ¼ cup of freshly brewed strong coffee or espresso into each glass and top off with the milky chai mixture.

Note:

For the espresso in this recipe, I've been known to use the instant stuff and I've yet to get any complaints.

Matcha Honey Latte

SERVES 8

3 tablespoons matcha powder
6 cups boiling water, divided
½ vanilla bean, split and scraped
½ cup liquid honey
3 cups milk

Everyone has heard the saying that opposites attract, right? Well, this latte is proof that it doesn't only apply to the world of dating. Bright green matcha finally meets its match here in the shape of flowery honey. The two complement each other, with the bitterness from the tea and those too-perfumey notes sometimes found in honey balancing each other out. Mixed with the dark muskiness of the vanilla bean and a creamy hit of whole milk, this is a *match-a* made in heaven.

In a large pot, whisk the matcha powder into ½ cup of the boiling water. Add in the vanilla bean pod and seeds, followed by the honey, and whisk to dissolve and combine. Whisk in the remaining 5 ½ cups of boiling water and the milk.

For hot lattes, place the pot over low heat and bring the mixture up to your preferred drinking temperature.

For iced lattes, pour the mixture over ice.

Getting ahead:
A batch of Matcha Honey Lattes can be stored in the fridge for up to 1 week in a pitcher or in mason jars. Before serving, give it a good stir or shake and serve cold over ice or reheat over low heat.

Bourbon Sweet Tea

SERVES 8

- 6 orange pekoe tea bags
- 4 cups boiling water
- ½ cup granulated sugar
- 2 cups bourbon
- ½ cup lemon juice (2–3 lemons)
- 2 teaspoons grated lemon zest
- Ice, lemon wedges or twist, and fresh mint leaves, for serving

SEE IMAGE ON PAGE 39

Ever since I was a wee baby with hair that stood straight up on my head like I was in some strange infant ska band, my family has taken a yearly vacation to Kiawah Island, South Carolina. I can still remember being so excited on the drive down, knowing we were getting close when I could see "sweet tea" on restaurant drink menus. It wasn't until later in life that I discovered another drink that the South is famous for. Bourbon and sweet tea are two of the many things that Southern cuisine gets so *so* right, and whipping the two into a brunchy cocktail makes me feel like I'm down South, sitting on a veranda, fanning away all that humidity and crossing my fingers that my hair will cooperate.

Steep the tea bags in the heated water for 7 to 9 minutes, depending on how strong you like your tea.

Meanwhile, in a small pot, combine 1 cup of water with the sugar and bring it to a boil. Boil until the sugar is dissolved, about 5 to 7 minutes. Stir the syrup into the tea, allow it to come to room temperature, and transfer the tea into a pitcher or large jar. Place the tea in the fridge to chill completely.

To serve, combine the sweetened tea with the bourbon, lemon juice, and zest in a large pitcher. Serve with ice, lemon, and a few fresh mint leaves.

Note:
When removing tea bags from water, do not squeeze them, as that will release too many tannins and give you bitter tea.

Chili Cucumber Lemonade

SERVES 8–10

- 1¾ cups granulated sugar
- 5–7 Thai chilies, plus extra for garnish
- 2 tablespoons grated lemon zest
- 1½ cups lemon juice (about 6 lemons)
- ½ cucumber, thinly sliced
- 1 lemon, thinly sliced
- Ice cubes
- 1½–1¾ cups gin (optional)

When I was a kid, my favorite thing about summer was setting up a lemonade stand. I remember one hot summer day when a girl roller-skated by and I was *so* disappointed that she didn't stop. Fast-forward 10 minutes to the sound of a dozen roller-skaters rolling up to my stand. She had wrangled all of her friends, and they guzzled down every last drop! To this day, lemonade continues to be my go-to summer drink, but, for a party, grown-up Mary digs some supporting characters tossed into the mix.

In a medium pot, combine 1 cup of water with the sugar. Toss in the Thai chilies and lemon zest, give it all a stir, and place the pot over medium heat. Bring the mixture to a simmer and cook until all of the sugar has dissolved, about 5 to 10 minutes. Remove the syrup from the heat and allow the chilies to steep for 5 to 10 minutes, depending on your spice tolerance.

Strain the syrup through a fine mesh sieve into a large pitcher and top with the lemon juice and 7 cups of cold water. Add in the cucumber and lemon slices and give everything a good stir before popping the lemonade in the fridge to cool completely.

To serve, fill your glasses with ice cubes and garnish with a fresh Thai chili in each. Top with 3 tablespoons of gin (if using), followed by the chilled chili cucumber lemonade.

Note:
I love to use Hendricks or another cucumber-y gin for this recipe, but a more juniper-forward variety will still be delicious.

Asparagus Zucchini Souffléd Omelet

SERVES 8

- 1 bundle asparagus, woody ends trimmed
- 1 zucchini, thinly sliced
- 2 cloves garlic, chopped
- 1 tablespoon olive oil
- 12 eggs, separated
- 1 teaspoon kosher salt
- ½ teaspoon freshly ground black pepper
- 4 oz soft goat cheese

Note:
In place of a stand mixer, you can use large clean metal or glass bowls and a hand mixer to whip your egg whites and yolks.

I'm not going to beat around the bush here: I kind of hate omelets. They always seem like a good idea, but I often end up with a rumpled, flattish egg thing filled with undercooked vegetables, wilted no-longer-green greens, and overcooked eggs. But there is hope! This here is my recipe for the most perfect omelet you'll ever have the joy of whipping up. Roasting the veggies makes them perfectly tender and flavorful. If the soufflé aspect of this recipe seems a bit intimidating, rest assured that it's as easy as anything. Perfect for a crowd or halved for a few, this is going to change your omelet game.

Preheat the oven to 400°F and scatter the asparagus, zucchini, and garlic across the bottom of a 9- × 13-inch ovenproof serving dish. Drizzle the vegetables with the oil and season with a pinch of salt and pepper.

Roast until slightly golden and tender, about 15 to 20 minutes. Remove the veg from the oven and transfer them to a plate. Leave the oven on. Spray the same ovenproof dish with a little nonstick cooking spray and set aside while you whip your eggs.

In a stand mixer fitted with the whip attachment, whip the egg whites with the salt until stiff peaks form, about 2 minutes, then transfer the whites to a clean metal or glass bowl.

Add the yolks and pepper to the bowl of a stand mixer and whip until pale and very airy, about 2 minutes. Remove the bowl from the mixer, scoop about one-third of the whites into the yolks, and gently but quickly whisk them in by hand. This first addition is meant to lighten the yolk mixture and, when you use a whisk, fewer of the air bubbles will burst.

Add in the remaining whites and use a spatula to gently fold the eggs together, being careful not to lose too much of that lovely loftiness.

Gently pour the eggs into the prepared dish, lightly drape the roasted vegetables over top, and dot with the goat cheese. Pop the omelet into the hot oven for about 15 to 18 minutes, or until the eggs are puffy, golden brown, and just set.

Serve straight away for optimal puffiness, but if it falls a bit, no worries. It'll still be delish.

Cheats Benny

SERVES 8

FOR THE HOLLANDAISE

8 egg yolks

3 tablespoons lemon juice

1 cup unsalted butter

1 teaspoon kosher salt

¼ teaspoon cayenne pepper

FOR THE POACHED EGGS

16 very fresh eggs

2 teaspoons white vinegar

1½ teaspoons kosher salt

FOR SERVING

8 English muffins, split and toasted

Bacon, Canadian bacon, smoked salmon, avocado, spinach, or whatever else your heart desires

Even though eggs Benedict is a brunch staple for so many, it has pretty much been relegated to professional kitchens, where a team of well-seasoned cooks work together to make one luxurious plate. Well, I'm here with some kitchen wizardry to help even the most cooking-averse whip up the perfect hollandaise to drape over beautifully poached eggs right in their own home, lickety-split! This recipe might seem a bit lengthy, but do not be deterred. It's filled with tips, tricks, and pointers to help you to expertly prepare eggs Benedict whether for a few or for a crowd. Just be sure to start with the freshest eggs you can find and you'll be golden.

For the hollandaise, place the egg yolks and lemon juice in a blender. Microwave the butter in 30-second increments in a heatproof glass measuring cup with a spout until it is melted and very hot, about 1 to 2 minutes. Turn the blender speed to high and remove the vent cap from the center of the lid. With the blender running, slowly stream the hot butter into the egg yolks. Season with the salt and cayenne pepper, taste, and adjust the seasoning if necessary.

If the consistency is a little thick for your liking, turn the blender back on and add some water, about 1 tablespoon at a time, until you reach your desired texture. To keep the hollandaise hot, transfer it to a glass or metal bowl and place it over a pot of barely simmering water. Give it a stir every once in a while to make sure it doesn't separate or appear curdled. If you do happen to split the hollandaise, pop it back in the blender, add 1 tablespoon of cold water, and blend on high speed until it's thick and creamy again.

For the poached eggs, place a large pot over medium heat and bring 4 inches of water to a simmer.

Meanwhile, crack 1 egg into a fine mesh sieve and gently jiggle it around a little. This will allow any runny bits of egg white to drain off, leaving you with just the yolk and firm part of the white. This removes the need to swirl your water when poaching the eggs and allows you to cook more eggs at once. Gently tip your egg into a heatproof bowl and continue with the rest of your eggs, adding them to the bowl as you go.

Note:

To get ahead, try poaching your eggs in advance. After removing the eggs from the pot, gently place them in a bowl of ice water to stop the cooking process. Keep the eggs in the ice water, cover, and refrigerate for up to 5 days. To reheat, bring a pot of water to a simmer and retrieve the eggs from the fridge. Slip the eggs into the simmering water for about 1 minute, then serve.

When the water has reached a simmer, add in the vinegar and salt. Gently tip 4 to 8 eggs into the simmering water, spacing them evenly around the pot. Cook the eggs for 3 to 4 minutes, depending on how runny you like your yolks. Personally, I'm a 3½-minute girl. That gives me a yolk that is halfway between runny and creamy. When the eggs are done to your liking, use a slotted spoon to scoop them out of the water and gently place them on a piece of paper towel to drain. Continue cooking the eggs until they are all done and then serve them on the toasted English muffins, topped however you see fit. Spoon over that lovely hollandaise and put any extra into a gravy boat to set out on the table for your more gluttonous guests (i.e., me).

Maple Candied Bacon

SERVES 8–10

24–26 oz thick-cut bacon (about 25–30 slices)
½ cup pure maple syrup
1 teaspoon coarsely ground black pepper

The whole reason I started cutting meat out of my diet is because of bacon. It's not that I hated the stuff—quite the opposite, in fact. I practically lived on bacon as a child, and by the ripe old age of 12 I felt that I had eaten more of the stuff than any normal person should throughout their whole life. At around 16 years old, I cut it out of my diet, but when I did indulge in that crispy, smoky breakfast staple, maple bacon was always my favorite. This recipe goes out to that tiny bacon maniac from my past.

Preheat your oven to 400°F and line a large baking sheet with aluminum foil. Lay the bacon out in a single layer and bake for 15 minutes, or until cooked but still a bit wobbly. Remove the bacon from the oven, transfer it to a large bowl, and toss it with the maple syrup. Pour off any excess grease from the pan, place the bacon back onto the sheet, and sprinkle it evenly with pepper. Bake the bacon until it is crisp and the syrup has candied onto it, making it a little tacky, about 5 to 10 minutes. Serve as a smoky sweet side to any of your favorite breakfasts or enjoy all on its own.

Croque Monsieur

SERVES 8

¼ cup unsalted butter
4¼ cups milk
½ cup all-purpose flour
2 teaspoons kosher salt
½ teaspoon freshly ground black pepper
1 teaspoon herbes de Provence
⅛ teaspoon nutmeg, freshly grated or ground
1 cup grated Pecorino Romano cheese
5 cups grated Gruyère cheese, divided
16 slices country bread
2½ tablespoons smooth Dijon mustard
10 oz thinly sliced ham or smoked salmon (optional)

Note:

The béchamel can be made up to 4 days in advance if stored in an airtight container in the fridge, and the sandwiches can be fully assembled and placed in the fridge for up to 5 hours before they go in the oven. If you have premade the béchamel or preassembled the sandwiches, increase the initial baking time to 6 to 8 minutes, followed by a 3-minute broil.

I can still remember when I was introduced to this French classic. I was 16, gallivanting around the restaurants of Strasbourg, France, and thinking myself very fancy ordering what is essentially a snazzed-up version of grilled cheese. After my first bite, I could almost hear angels singing. The combination of toasted country bread, rich béchamel, nutty Gruyère, and Dijon is so much more than the sum of its parts, and I guarantee that this will become an instant classic on your table.

Preheat your oven to 400°F and position an oven rack in the center of the oven.

To make the béchamel, melt the butter in a large pot over medium heat. While the butter is melting, heat the milk in a separate pot over medium-low heat or microwave it for 1 to 2 minutes, or until it's quite warm but not boiling.

When the butter is melted, sprinkle the flour over top and whisk in. Cook over medium heat, whisking constantly, for 2 to 3 minutes, until the mixture just starts to turn a light golden color. Continuing to whisk, slowly pour in the warmed milk and season the mixture with the salt, pepper, herbes de Provence, and nutmeg. Cook, stirring occasionally, until the mixture is thick, creamy, and coats the back of a spoon.

Once thick, whisk in the Pecorino Romano and 1 cup of the Gruyère. Keep it over low heat so that it stays warm.

Meanwhile, very lightly toast the bread and lay it out on a baking sheet. Spread the Dijon over half of the slices and top with ham or salmon (if using). Spread about 3 to 4 tablespoons of the béchamel on top and sprinkle each with ¼ cup of Gruyère. Top each with a plain slice of toast, 3 to 4 tablespoons of béchamel, and another ¼ cup of Gruyère. Bake for 4 minutes.

Turn on the broiler and, leaving the baking sheet in the center of the oven, broil for 3 minutes, or until the top of the sandwiches are golden and bubbling.

Serve hot from the oven, seasoned with salt and pepper to taste.

Shakshuka Puttanesca

SERVES 6–8

2 tablespoons olive oil
1 cooking onion, finely diced
2 cloves garlic, finely minced
½ red bell pepper, diced
1 pint cherry tomatoes, halved
2 tablespoons tomato paste
Kosher salt
2 tablespoons vodka
1 tablespoon granulated sugar
1 (28 oz) can crushed tomatoes
8 anchovy fillets, finely minced
1 teaspoon smoked paprika
½ teaspoon dried chili flakes
½ cup chopped kalamata olives
½ cup flat-leaf parsley, plus more for garnish
¼ cup fresh basil, plus more for garnish
2 tablespoons capers
1 tablespoon lemon juice
2 teaspoons smooth Dijon mustard
8–12 eggs
5–7 oz feta cheese
Pita bread, warmed, for serving

Meet my dream food baby: Shakshuka Puttanesca. Not only is the name a hoot to say, but the blending of these two classic dishes somehow works *so* well. By adding puttanesca's anchovies, capers, and olives to the classic flavors of shakshuka, you end up with a dish that is so satisfyingly good and perfectly balanced. It's salty, saucy, sweet, spicy, anchovy-y, eggy, and just on the right side of wrong. It's simply perfect for breakfast, brunch, lunch, dinner, hangovers, parties, and everything in between.

In a large sauté pan or frying pan with a tight-fitting lid, warm the oil over medium-low heat. Cook the onions, garlic, and bell peppers until soft and starting to lightly caramelize, about 5 to 7 minutes. Add in the cherry tomatoes and tomato paste and season with a bit of salt. Cook for another 3 minutes or so and then add in the vodka and sugar, followed by the crushed tomatoes, anchovies, smoked paprika, and chili flakes. Pop the lid on the pan and turn down the heat to low. Allow the sauce to simmer away for 20 to 25 minutes to develop the flavors.

When you're ready to poach the eggs, stir in the olives, parsley, basil, capers, lemon juice, and Dijon. Crack the eggs into the sauce, pop the lid back on, and simmer for 6 to 8 minutes, or until the whites of the eggs are set and the yolks are still lovely and runny.

Scatter some parsley, basil, and feta on top to garnish and serve alongside some warmed pita.

Chorizo, Kale, and Butternut Squash Strata

SERVES 10-12

- 1 small butternut squash, peeled, seeded, and cut into 1-inch chunks
- 2½ tablespoons olive oil, divided
- 1 teaspoon Italian seasoning
- 1 head garlic
- 8 oz chorizo sausage
- 12 eggs
- 3 cups milk
- 2 teaspoons smoked paprika
- 1½ teaspoons kosher salt
- ½ teaspoon freshly ground black pepper
- ½ teaspoon cayenne pepper
- 1 loaf sourdough bread, cubed
- 3 cups kale, stems removed and finely chopped
- 3 cups grated Manchego or Parmigiano-Reggiano cheese

When I was growing up, Easter was always a pretty big deal at my church. On Palm Sunday, bushels of palm leaves would be delivered, and all of the kids would weave baskets, twist little roses, and braid crosses. The following Friday, the church hosted a Good Friday breakfast—I looked forward to it every year. As all good church breakfasts should be, it was basically just a strata-fest made up of classic bacon, egg, and cheddar cheese bakes. I think that is where my love of those rich, savory bread puddings began. This is a more flavorful version of the classic, but it's just as easy and perfect for a stress-free brunch any day of the year.

Preheat your oven to 400°F and prepare your butternut squash by tossing it onto a baking sheet and drizzling with 2 tablespoons of the olive oil. Season it with a bit of salt, pepper, and the Italian seasoning and set aside. Prepare the garlic for roasting by removing any loose papery layers from the skin and trimming about ¼ inch from the top of the head to expose the cloves. Place it on a piece of aluminum foil and drizzle it with the remaining ½ tablespoon of olive oil. Wrap the foil around the garlic and roast it, along with the butternut squash, for 20 to 25 minutes, or until the squash is nicely caramelized and the garlic is soft and golden.

Meanwhile, heat a frying pan over medium heat. Remove the chorizo from its casing, crumble it into the pan, and cook for about 8 to 10 minutes, stirring occasionally, until golden and cooked through. Remove the chorizo from the pan and set aside to cool.

In a large bowl, beat the eggs and add in the milk, paprika, salt, pepper, and cayenne. Squeeze 4 cloves of the roasted garlic out of the bulb, give them a bit of a mash, and whisk them into the egg mixture.

Lightly grease a 10- × 15-inch deep-sided casserole dish and scatter half of the bread across the bottom of it. Top with half of the cooled butternut squash, chorizo, kale, and grated cheese. Repeat these layers, omitting the cheese layer this time, and pour the egg mixture evenly over top. Scatter the remaining cheese on top, cover with aluminum foil dull side down, and chill overnight.

When you're ready to bake, remove the strata from the fridge while you preheat the oven to 375°F. Keep the foil on the strata and bake for 25 minutes, then remove the foil and continue to bake for another 25 to 30 minutes, or until the center of the strata is set and the cheese is golden brown.

Leek Babka

MAKES ONE 9- X 5-INCH LOAF

FOR THE BREAD

½ cup milk

¾ cup warm water

1 tablespoon liquid honey

2¼–2¾ cups bread flour (see note)

1½ tablespoons milk powder

2½ teaspoons instant/rapid-rise yeast

2 teaspoons kosher salt

1 egg, beaten

2 tablespoons unsalted butter, melted

1 egg + 2 teaspoons milk, for egg wash

FOR THE FILLING

3 tablespoons unsalted butter

2 leeks, trimmed, halved, washed, and very thinly sliced

1 clove garlic, minced

1 tablespoon chopped flat-leaf parsley

1 teaspoon chopped fresh thyme leaves

1 tablespoon lemon juice

1 teaspoon grated lemon zest

½ teaspoon kosher salt

½ teaspoon freshly ground black pepper

4½ oz soft goat cheese

½ cup finely grated Parmigiano-Reggiano cheese

Leeks are probably the most underrated member of the allium family, and I think it's about time they got their time in the spotlight! Their buttery, mellow flavor lends itself perfectly to stocks, poultry, eggs, or, in this case, bread. To really let them shine, I decided to roll them up in a buttery milk dough, slice it down the center, and twist it all up into a babka. It's the perfect addition to any table, but I like mine with breakfast—it gets the day off to a great start.

For the bread, heat the milk in a pot over medium heat on the stove or in the microwave until very warm but not simmering. Stir in the warm water and honey and set aside for a few minutes to cool slightly.

Meanwhile, combine 2¼ cups of the bread flour, the milk powder, yeast, and salt in the bowl of a stand mixer fitted with the dough hook. Pour in the warm milk and honey mixture, followed by the egg and butter, and knead with the dough hook for 5 to 6 minutes. If the dough continues to be quite sticky and pool at the bottom of the bowl, gradually add in more flour and knead until it comes together and starts to climb the dough hook. Remove the hook and cover the bowl with plastic wrap and a tea towel. Allow the dough to rise in a warm spot for about 1 hour, or until doubled in size.

For the filling, melt the butter in a large frying pan over medium-low heat and sweat the leeks until soft, about 5 to 7 minutes. Add in the garlic, parsley, and thyme, and continue to cook for another 5 minutes. Remove the pan from the heat, stir in the lemon juice and zest and season with the salt and pepper. Cool the leeks to room temperature. Lightly grease a 9- × 5-inch loaf pan and set aside.

When the dough has risen, turn it out onto a lightly floured work surface and roll it out into a 12- × 15-inch rectangle. Evenly spread the leeks on top, dot with the goat cheese, and scatter the Parmigiano-Reggiano in an even layer over top. Starting with a long edge, tightly roll the dough into a snake (see fig. 1 on the following page) and seal the seam by pinching the dough together. Using a sharp knife, split the roll down the middle lengthwise (fig. 2) and twist the babka together (fig. 3). Place the loaf in the greased loaf pan, cover loosely with plastic wrap,

SEE STEP-BY-STEP IMAGES ON FOLLOWING PAGE

and drape with a tea towel. Allow the loaf to rise in a warm spot for 1 hour so that the top of the dough reaches above the edge of the loaf pan. About halfway through this second rise, preheat the oven to 375°F. Once the dough has risen, remove the plastic wrap and tea towel, gently brush the loaf with the egg wash, and bake for 40 to 50 minutes, or until the internal temperature reaches 200°F.

Allow the babka to cool in the pan for 10 minutes and then place it on a wire rack to cool completely.

Note:
On humid days, bread recipes might require more flour than indicated in the recipe. Don't be scared to slowly add more flour until the dough comes together, is less sticky, and starts to look like a ball of dough.

1

2

STEPS FOR LEEK BABKA (PAGE 36)

OPPOSITE: FRIED CHICKEN AND CORNMEAL WAFFLES WITH SPICY MAPLE SYRUP (PAGE 40) AND BOURBON SWEET TEA (PAGE 22)

3

Fried Chicken and Cornmeal Waffles with Spicy Maple Syrup

SERVES 8

FOR THE CHICKEN

8 bone-in, skin-on chicken thighs
8 bone-in, skin-on chicken drumsticks
3 cups buttermilk
3 teaspoons smoked paprika, divided
2½ teaspoons cayenne pepper, divided
2 teaspoons garlic powder
4 teaspoons kosher salt, divided
1½ teaspoons freshly ground black pepper, divided
2½ cups all-purpose flour
Vegetable oil, for frying

FOR THE CORNMEAL WAFFLES

1½ cups all-purpose flour
1 cup yellow cornmeal
1 tablespoon granulated sugar
1 tablespoon baking powder
1 teaspoon baking soda
½ teaspoon kosher salt
2 eggs
2 cups buttermilk
¼ cup unsalted butter, melted
¼ cup finely chopped chives

FOR THE SPICY MAPLE SYRUP

1 cup pure maple syrup
½ teaspoon smoked paprika
½ teaspoon cayenne pepper
½ teaspoon freshly ground black pepper

When I was on *MasterChef Canada*, for one challenge we were asked to create a dish that represented our families. It was down to four home cooks and the pressure was getting pretty intense. When we left the pantry, we were all shocked and delighted to find our families waiting to take us shopping for the ingredients we would need to create our family-inspired dish. While the other home cooks chose to create elevated versions of their culinary heritage, my mind jumped immediately to Southern cuisine. My family isn't from the South—we mainly hail from Canada's East Coast—but there is something about Southern food that screams "family" to me. It might boil down to our long drives south to visit my nana or our family vacations to South Carolina, but for this challenge, the only thing on my mind was chicken and waffles—a Berg favorite and the ultimate Southern breakfast.

For the chicken, place the chicken thighs and drumsticks in a large resealable plastic bag and pour in the buttermilk. Add in 2 teaspoons of the smoked paprika, 2 teaspoons of the cayenne, the garlic powder, 3 teaspoons of the salt, and 1 teaspoon of the black pepper and mash it all around to evenly distribute the spices. Seal the bag, removing as much air as possible, and place it in a large bowl or baking pan in order to catch any potential leaks. Place the chicken in the fridge overnight, or for up to 24 hours, to marinate.

When you're ready to fry, preheat your oven to 350°F, place a wire rack over a baking sheet, and remove the chicken from the fridge.

In a large bowl, combine the all-purpose flour with the remaining 1 teaspoon of smoked paprika, ½ teaspoon of cayenne, 1 teaspoon of salt, and ½ teaspoon of black pepper and whisk to combine. Remove the chicken pieces from the buttermilk and coat each piece thoroughly with the flour mixture, shaking off any excess. Set the chicken out on the prepared rack and allow it to rest for 20 to 25 minutes.

Heat 1 inch of vegetable oil in a large, heavy-bottomed pot or cast iron skillet over medium heat until it reaches 365°F. If you don't have a kitchen thermometer, place the end of a wooden spoon in the oil to test it. If bubbles form immediately, the oil is ready for frying.

While the oil heats, dredge the chicken pieces once more in the flour mixture and return to the rack. When the oil is hot, work in batches of about 4 pieces at a time to fry the chicken for 5 minutes per side, or until the coating is a lovely golden brown. Use kitchen tongs to remove the chicken from the oil and place it on the rack-lined sheet. When all of the chicken has been fried, transfer it to the oven and bake for 30 to 35 minutes, or until the internal temperature reaches 160°F to 165°F.

While the chicken finishes cooking in the oven, make your waffles. Preheat a waffle iron or a ridged griddle pan over medium heat. Combine the flour, cornmeal, sugar, baking powder, baking soda, and salt in a large bowl. Whisk these together and then add in the eggs, buttermilk, butter, and chives. Whisk just until combined.

If you're using a waffle iron, spritz the inside with a little nonstick cooking spray and pour about ½ cup of batter into the center of the iron. Close and cook until golden and crispy. If you're using a ridged griddle pan, simply grease it and pour ½ cup of your batter onto the pan as you would pancakes and cook for 2 to 3 minutes per side. Wrap your cooked waffles in a towel to keep them warm.

For the syrup, combine the maple syrup, smoked paprika, cayenne, and pepper in a microwave-safe dish. Microwave for 30 seconds to 1 minute, or until warm.

Serve the waffles topped with the chicken and drizzled with spicy maple syrup.

Carbonara Pizza

SERVES 8–10

- 1 (1½ lb) ball store-bought pizza dough
- 6–7 oz thick-cut pancetta or guanciale, diced
- 2 tablespoons olive oil
- 1 clove garlic, minced
- ¼ cup + 2 tablespoons finely chopped flat-leaf parsley, divided
- Kosher salt
- 1 teaspoon coarsely ground black pepper, divided
- 3–4 cups shredded mozzarella cheese
- 1 cup finely grated Pecorino Romano cheese
- 8 egg yolks

It's a universally accepted fact that pizza and pasta are traditionally later-in-the-day foods. But I got to thinking one day about what it would look like to combine some key breakfast flavors—eggs, cheese, bacon—into a dish that turned dinner into breakfast. Spaghetti carbonara is essentially all of breakfast's key players tossed onto some noodles. And who hasn't grabbed a cold slice of pizza from the fridge on a busy morning? I say let's bring the two together and create the world's most amazing early morning–approved 'za that doesn't make you feel like a university student rushing out the door to get to an 8:00 a.m. class.

Preheat your oven to 475°F, lightly grease two baking sheets, and remove the pizza dough from the fridge to allow it to come to room temperature.

In a medium frying pan over medium heat, cook the pancetta (or guanciale) until crisp. Remove the meat from the pan, reserving the fat. Add the olive oil to the fat and allow it to warm over medium-low heat.

Toss in the garlic and cook for about 1 minute. Pour the fat and garlic mixture into a small heatproof bowl and add in the ¼ cup of parsley. Season with a pinch of salt and ½ teaspoon of the pepper and set aside.

Divide your pizza dough in half and stretch each half into a large, thin circle. Place the dough on the prepared baking sheets and divide the garlic oil over each. Using the back of a spoon, spread the oil out so that it coats almost the whole top of each pizza, leaving just a little room around the edges for the crust.

Scatter the top of the pizzas with both cheeses. Dot the cooked pancetta (or guanciale) over top of each pizza and bake for 10 to 15 minutes, or until the cheese is golden and bubbly and the crust is crisp.

Remove the pizzas from the oven and gently top each one with 4 egg yolks. Place the pizzas back in the oven for 1 minute, just to slightly set the yolks.

When the pizzas are done, scatter the remaining parsley, pepper, and a bit of salt over top of each. Cut each pizza into 8 or 10 slices, being sure to cut through the yolks so that they break and ooze everywhere.

Grilled Cheese with Quick Blackberry Rosemary Freezer Jam

SERVES 8 (WITH LOTS OF LEFTOVER JAM)

FOR THE JAM

2 cups fresh blackberries
2 tablespoons lemon juice
¼ cup (1 package) pectin crystals
1 cup superfine sugar
½ cup light corn syrup
2 sprigs rosemary
½ teaspoon pure vanilla extract

FOR THE GRILLED CHEESE

16 slices good, tasty bread
½ cup salted butter
14–16 oz Brie cheese, sliced
½ cup Quick Blackberry Rosemary Freezer Jam (or store-bought blackberry jam)

Note:
If you're looking to get ahead, feel free to assemble the sandwiches a few hours early, or even the night before. Tightly covered, they will hold up in the fridge and taste scrumptious grilled just before serving.

When I was a kid, grilled cheese meant one thing and one thing only: lighter-than-air white bread, wiggly processed cheese slices, and way too much ketchup. While the classic still holds a special place in my heart, my tastes have evolved a little since then. My current fave is almost like a cheeseboard in sandwich form. Homemade blackberry freezer jam infused with rosemary, slathered on some hearty bread like sourdough or something super seedy, topped with oozy Brie. Feel free to use store-bought jam, but this freezer jam is a breeze to make and a dream to eat. I'm a fan of dipping, and nothing beats grainy Dijon with this sammy.

For the jam, place the blackberries and lemon juice in a large pot and, using a potato masher, roughly mash up the blackberries. Evenly sprinkle the pectin crystals over top of the berries and give the whole mixture a stir. Allow this to sit at room temperature for 30 minutes, giving it a gentle mix every 10 minutes or so.

Stir in the sugar, corn syrup, and rosemary and place the pot over medium heat. Bring the mixture to a simmer and cook the jam for 5 minutes, without stirring, just to help break down the sugar and allow the rosemary flavor to get to know those juicy blackberries.

Remove the jam from the heat, stir in the vanilla extract, and divide the jam between three clean 1-cup jars. Allow the jam to come to room temperature, seal the jars, place two of them in the freezer so that they will keep longer, and store one in the fridge for immediate use.

Preheat your oven to 200°F.

For the grilled cheese, butter one side of each piece of bread and flip half of them over, leaving 8 slices butter side up and 8 butter side down. Spread each of the butter-side-down slices with 1 tablespoon of jam and top with sliced pieces of Brie. Sandwich everything together with the remaining slices of bread, butter sides out, and cook in a nonstick frying pan over medium heat until golden brown, about 2 to 3 minutes per side. Keep the sandwiches warm in the oven until ready to serve.

Shrimp, Sprout, and Avocado Croissants

SERVES 8

- 8 good-quality croissants
- 4 cups diced medium-size cooked shrimp
- ½–¾ cup mayonnaise
- 1½ tablespoons lemon juice
- 2 teaspoons grated lemon zest
- 3 tablespoons finely chopped chives
- 3 tablespoons finely chopped flat-leaf parsley
- Kosher salt
- Freshly ground black pepper
- 2 avocados, sliced
- 2 cups alfalfa sprouts, lightly packed

There used to be this little bakery in Toronto, right across from Trinity Bellwoods Park, that made the world's best croissants. Plain, filled, or stuffed, every single one was amazing. I could never walk by without stopping in to see if my favorite combination was on the menu. If it wasn't, I could always be persuaded to pick up one or two of their sweet varieties like the peanut butter, chocolate, banana, or fig to comfort me. Don't get me wrong, all of their croissants were worth a visit, but the mishmash of little pink shrimp, frizzly sprouts, and creamy avocado just called to me!

Using a serrated knife, split the croissants in half, leaving a hinge on one side like a hot dog bun.

Dry the chopped shrimp well with paper towel in order to absorb as much liquid as possible. This will help the croissant hold together. In a medium bowl, combine the shrimp, mayonnaise, lemon juice, zest, chives, parsley, and a bit of salt and pepper to taste. Fill each croissant with a few slices of avocado, ¼ cup of alfalfa sprouts, and ½ cup of the shrimp salad.

Finish with a little more salt and pepper and you've got the tastiest sandwiches anyone ever did see.

Note:
For good-quality croissants, I always recommend checking out a local bakery. There you can often find crisp and flaky croissants, which are perfect for this recipe.

Coconut Pecan Granola with Bourbon-Stewed Peaches

SERVES 8 (WITH A BOATLOAD OF LEFTOVER GRANOLA)

FOR THE GRANOLA

4 cups rolled oats
2 cups pecans, halves or chopped
1 cup sweetened shredded coconut
½ cup ground flax seed
¼ cup brown sugar, packed
2 tablespoons all-purpose flour
1 teaspoon kosher salt
½ cup boiling water
½ cup pure maple syrup
¼ cup vegetable oil
2 teaspoons pure vanilla extract

FOR THE PEACHES

10–12 peaches, pits removed and chopped into large chunks
¼ cup brown sugar, packed
½ teaspoon ground cinnamon
¼ cup pure maple syrup
2 tablespoons bourbon
2 teaspoons lemon juice
2 tablespoons unsalted butter
1 teaspoon pure vanilla extract

Oh, how I love granola. It's crunchy, nutty, super easy to make and, with a little imagination, can be used in so many different dishes. This one in particular, served with some lovely bourbon-stewed peaches, is exceptionally delicious served on yogurt for a creamy and crunchy breakfast or scooped and scattered over a bowl of pralines and creamy ice cream for dessert. It's healthy, high in fiber, and gives a nod to the South with its flavors of coconut, pecans, peaches, and good old-fashioned bourbon.

Preheat your oven to 300°F.

In a large bowl, mix together the oats, pecans, coconut, flax seed, sugar, flour, and salt, giving it a good stir to evenly combine. In a large measuring cup or small bowl, place the water, maple syrup, oil, and vanilla. Whisk together to combine, then add the wet ingredients to the oat mixture. Stir thoroughly to ensure that every little morsel is evenly coated.

Spread the granola onto a large baking sheet and bake it for 1 hour and 20 minutes, stirring every 20 minutes or so, until the granola has crisped up and is lightly golden brown.

Meanwhile, whip up the stewed peaches by combining the peaches, brown sugar, cinnamon, syrup, bourbon, lemon juice, and butter in a large pot over medium-high heat. Give the mixture a stir and bring it to a boil. Turn down the heat to a simmer and cook, stirring occasionally, for 15 to 20 minutes, or until the peaches are tender and starting to break down. Stir in the vanilla and set the peaches aside to cool.

When the granola is golden and crisp, allow it to cool completely before serving with the bourbon-stewed peaches. The granola will stay delicious stored at room temperature in an airtight container for a good long while, but in my house it rarely lasts longer than a couple of weeks.

Baked Steel Cut Oatmeal

SERVES 8–10

¼ cup unsalted butter
1½ cups steel cut oats
½ cup sliced almonds
3 tablespoons ground flax seed
1 egg
3 cups milk
¾ cup buttermilk
½ cup pure maple syrup
2 teaspoons pure vanilla extract
2–3 teaspoons ground cinnamon
2 teaspoons baking powder
¾ teaspoon kosher salt
Fresh or stewed fruit, for serving

Oatmeal is one of those things that never really gets its time in the spotlight. I feel like as soon as someone mentions the stuff, images of boxes and little brown paper bags of instant mush come to mind and, while those are convenient for a quick weekday breakfast, they don't do the humble oat justice. For me, the king of oats is the steel cut oat. It's chewy, nutty, and super healthy, and, if you prepare it like this, it makes one heck of a breakfast for a crowd.

Preheat your oven to 375°F and position an oven rack in the center of the oven.

In a large cast iron skillet, melt the butter over medium heat. Add in the oats, almonds, and flax seed and stir to combine. Toast the mixture in the pan for about 2 minutes, or until everything starts to smell nice and nutty.

Meanwhile, beat the egg in a large bowl and then beat in the milk, buttermilk, maple syrup, vanilla, cinnamon (to taste), baking powder, and salt.

Remove the skillet from the heat, carefully pour the milk mixture over the oats, give it a stir, and gently transfer the skillet to the oven. Bake the oatmeal for 45 to 55 minutes, or until set. All of the almonds will float to the top, giving you the loveliest crunchy topping and an almost pudding-y oatmeal.

Serve hot with fresh or stewed fruit.

Note:
This recipe is also the perfect prepped breakfast for your work week. Just whip up a batch on Sunday and dig in to an easy breakfast every workday morning.

Blueberry Cheesecake French Toast Bake with Apple Cinnamon Syrup

SERVES 8

FOR THE BREAD AND CUSTARD

16 thick slices French or egg bread
8 eggs
2 cups milk
½ cup 35% whipping cream
½ cup brown sugar, packed
2 teaspoons pure vanilla extract
2 teaspoons ground cinnamon
¼ teaspoon nutmeg, freshly grated or ground
½ teaspoon fine salt
1 cup fresh or frozen blueberries
¾ cup brick cream cheese, cut into small pieces
1 cup chopped pecans

FOR THE SYRUP

½ cup brown sugar, packed
2 tablespoons cornstarch
1 teaspoon ground cinnamon
⅛ teaspoon nutmeg, freshly grated or ground
1½ cups apple cider
2 tablespoons lemon juice
3 tablespoons unsalted butter

If making French toast for a crowd sounds like a nightmare, that's because it is. Frying any more than four slices at a time is a trick even Dumbledore would find difficult. Since I never received my letter to Hogwarts (wannabe Hufflepuffs, unite!) but I am a lady who loves French toast, here is a classic Berg family kitchen trick for the tastiest, easiest, most wizardly way to whip up French toast for a crowd. Just make sure you go that extra step and make the apple cinnamon syrup, because geezy louisey, is it ever good.

Lightly grease a 9- × 13-inch deep-sided casserole dish and set aside. Lay the slices of bread out on a wire rack to allow them to dry out while you prepare your custard.

In a large bowl, beat together the eggs, milk, cream, sugar, vanilla, cinnamon, nutmeg, and salt and set aside. Arrange the bread in the prepared dish and scatter with the blueberries, cream cheese, and finally the pecans, making sure to tuck some of each in between the slices of bread. Gently pour the custard over top and cover tightly with a piece of plastic wrap. Place the dish in the fridge and allow it to chill for at least 2 hours, or up to overnight.

When you're ready to bake, remove the dish from the fridge and preheat the oven to 375°F. Remove the plastic, tightly cover the dish with foil, and bake for 25 minutes. Remove the foil and continue to bake for 20 to 25 minutes, or until the bread is golden brown and set in the middle.

For the syrup, combine the brown sugar, cornstarch, cinnamon, and nutmeg in a small saucepan. Whisk in the apple cider and lemon juice and turn on the heat to medium. Bring the syrup to a simmer and cook, stirring frequently until the mixture has thickened, for about 8 to 10 minutes. Whisk in the butter and keep the syrup warm over low heat until ready to serve over the French toast bake.

Lemon Poppy Seed Dutch Babies

SERVES 8

- 1⅓ cups all-purpose flour
- 2 tablespoons granulated sugar
- 2 tablespoons poppy seeds
- ½ teaspoon kosher salt
- 6 eggs
- 1⅓ cups warm milk
- 1 tablespoon grated lemon zest
- 1 teaspoon pure vanilla extract
- 2 tablespoons vegetable oil, divided
- 2 tablespoons unsalted butter, divided
- Fresh berries, lemon wedges, icing sugar, butter, and pure maple syrup, for serving

My favorite place in the world is our little family cottage up on a lake in northern Ontario. It's the kind of place where afternoons are spent lazing about reading novels, dinners are usually a smorgasbord of whatever's in the fridge, and beers are cracked by around two o'clock in the afternoon. While most meals tend to be a bit haphazard, breakfast is always a production. Pancakes are a classic, but standing in front of the stove flipping while everyone else gets down to a rousing game of euchre is kind of a bummer. Luckily, Dutch babies are here to save the day.

Place two 9- or 10-inch cast iron skillets on the middle rack of your oven and preheat it to 450°F.

In a large bowl, combine the flour, sugar, poppy seeds, and salt. In a separate bowl, whisk together the eggs, milk, lemon zest, and vanilla. Whisk the wet ingredients into the dry and set aside.

When the oven has reached temperature, remove the skillets from the oven and place 1 tablespoon of both vegetable oil and butter into each. Carefully swirl them around to coat the bottom of each pan and quickly and carefully split the batter between the two skillets.

Place the skillets back in the oven, drop the temperature to 425°F, and bake for 12 to 15 minutes, or until the Dutch babies are ultra-puffy and golden brown.

Serve immediately, but don't worry when all of that puffiness starts to fall. The edges should stay tall and proud, leaving you with lots of room for berries, lemon juice, icing sugar, butter, and maple syrup.

Pistachio Raspberry Bostock

SERVES 8

FOR THE HONEY SIMPLE SYRUP

3 tablespoons granulated sugar
1 tablespoon liquid honey
¼ teaspoon pure vanilla extract

FOR THE PISTACHIO FRANGIPANE

2 cups shelled pistachios
¼ cup all-purpose flour
1 teaspoon kosher salt
½ cup unsalted butter
½ cup granulated sugar
3 tablespoons liquid honey
2 eggs
2 teaspoons pure vanilla extract

FOR THE ASSEMBLY

8 (each 1½ inches) slices brioche or good egg bread
½ cup raspberry jam
¼ cup chopped pistachios
Icing sugar

Easier, and arguably better, than classic French toast, bostock combines all of the staples of breakfast in one delicious meal: syrup, toast, jam, and more sugar than should probably be eaten first thing in the morning.

Preheat your oven to 350°F and lightly coat a baking sheet with nonstick cooking spray.

For the simple syrup, combine the sugar, honey, and vanilla with ¼ cup of water in a small pot and place over medium-high heat. Simmer the syrup until all of the sugar dissolves, about 5 to 6 minutes, then remove the pot from the heat and allow it to cool slightly.

For the pistachio frangipane, blitz the pistachios in a food processor until ground to the consistency of almond flour and transfer to a bowl. Stir in the flour and salt and set aside. In a bowl, cream the butter, sugar, and honey together using a rubber spatula or a wooden spoon. Once smooth, beat in the eggs, followed by the vanilla extract. Stir in the pistachio mixture until combined and set aside.

To assemble the bostock, lightly brush both sides of each slice of brioche (or egg bread) with the simple syrup, making sure to cover every inch. Place the slices down on your prepared baking sheet, leaving a couple of inches between each. Spread each slice with a slightly heaped tablespoon of raspberry jam followed by a heaping ¼ cup of the frangipane mixture. Scatter chopped pistachios on top and bake for 20 to 25 minutes, or until golden brown.

Serve the bostock hot or at room temperature, sprinkled with icing sugar and a drizzle of honey if you're feeling snazzy.

Note:

Traditional frangipane is made with almonds and is kind of like a custardy cousin to marzipan. This pistachio take on frangipane can be made up to 2 days ahead and the syrup lasts for up to 1 month stored in an airtight container in the fridge, so feel free to whip up these components in advance. That way, all you need to do to look like a culinary maven first thing in the morning is brush some syrup, spread some jam and such, and bake.

The Biggest Cinnamon Roll Ever with Vanilla Crème Fraîche

MAKES 1 GIANT CINNAMON ROLL (SERVES 8–12)

FOR THE VANILLA CRÈME FRAÎCHE

1 cup whipping (35%) cream
2 tablespoons buttermilk
1 vanilla bean, sliced and scraped

FOR THE DOUGH

¼ cup warm milk
2½ teaspoons instant/rapid-rise yeast
¼ cup granulated sugar
4 egg yolks
1 egg
¼ cup + 2 tablespoons unsalted butter, melted
½ cup buttermilk
1 teaspoon pure vanilla extract
3¼–4 cups all-purpose flour
1¼ teaspoons fine salt

FOR THE FILLING

¼ cup unsalted butter
1 cup brown sugar, packed
1 cup chopped pecans or walnuts
2 tablespoons ground cinnamon
⅛ teaspoon fine salt

I don't think anyone can resist the temptation of freshly baked cinnamon rolls. They are soft, spicy, sweet, and pretty much perfect in every way. In my mind, the only way to make a cinnamon roll better is to make it bigger and drown it in vanilla crème fraîche.

For the crème fraîche, combine the whipping cream and buttermilk in a small jar with a tight-fitting lid and give it a shake. Leave the jar out on the counter for 8 to 24 hours to thicken. I know that this sounds a little strange, but don't worry, you'll have delicious crème fraîche in no time!

Once it's thick, stir in the scraped vanilla seeds and store in the fridge, tightly covered, for up to 1 week.

For the cinnamon bun dough, stir together the warm milk and yeast in a small bowl. Set aside to allow the yeast to get to work and for the mixture to get foamy. In a stand mixer fitted with a whip attachment, whip the sugar with the egg yolks and whole egg until light and fluffy, about 2 minutes. Once fluffy, pour in the melted butter followed by the buttermilk and vanilla and whip to combine.

Remove the whip attachment from your mixer and add the yeast mixture as well as 3¼ cups of the flour and the salt. Holding the hook attachment in your hand, vigorously stir this mixture until it comes together. Once it's mixed, attach the dough hook to the stand mixer and knead the dough on low/medium-low speed for 5 minutes. At this point, the dough should be soft and moist but not sticky. If it's sticky, slowly add some more flour, ¼ cup at a time, until it no longer sticks to your hands. Whether or not you add more flour, continue to knead the dough on low for an additional 5 minutes until the dough is soft and springs back when poked.

Transfer the dough to a large, lightly greased bowl, cover with plastic wrap and a clean kitchen towel, and allow it to rise in a warm place for 1 hour, or until doubled in size.

While the dough is rising, mix up the filling by combining the butter with the brown sugar, nuts, cinnamon, and salt. Set aside.

Once your dough has risen, prepare a 10-inch round cake pan or cast iron skillet by evenly coating the bottom and sides with butter. Punch down the dough and roll it out on a floured work surface into a 13- × 20-inch rectangle. Evenly spread the filling mixture over the dough and, using a knife or pizza cutter, cut the dough into 10 equal strips along the long edge.

Roll one strip of dough into a coil and place it in the center of your prepared pan. Continue to coil the remaining strips around the center piece of dough so that you get a giant cinnamon roll swirl. Loosely cover the pan with plastic wrap and a clean kitchen towel and allow the dough to rise in a warm place for another hour until puffy.

Preheat your oven to 350°F and bake for 35 to 45 minutes, or until the center of the bun reaches 185°F.

Allow the bun to cool slightly, or all the way to room temperature, and drizzle with the crème fraîche to serve.

Note:
To reheat the cinnamon roll, brush the top with a bit of melted unsalted butter, cover tightly with aluminum foil, and place in a cold oven. Heat the oven to 300°F and then set a timer for 5 to 8 minutes. Remove from the oven and serve immediately, glazed with the vanilla crème fraîche.

Tiramisu Crêpe Cake

MAKES 1 (8-INCH) CAKE

FOR THE CRÊPES

2¼ cups all-purpose flour
2 tablespoons granulated sugar
¼ teaspoon fine salt
3 eggs
1½ cups milk
2 tablespoons unsalted butter, melted
2 teaspoons pure vanilla extract

FOR THE FILLING

1½ cups whipping (35%) cream
¼ cup + 2 tablespoons icing sugar
2 cups mascarpone cheese
2 tablespoons marsala wine
1 tablespoon pure vanilla extract
2 teaspoons instant espresso powder
¼ teaspoon fine salt

FOR THE ASSEMBLY

¼ cup cocoa powder
2 tablespoons icing sugar
1 cup fresh raspberries

When I was about 12 years old, I went through a serious crêpe phase. While all of the other neighborhood kids were busy getting dolled-up for preteen dances and *very* romantic hand holding, you could find me in the kitchen whipping up dozens of crêpes to fill with all things fruity, cheesy, saucy, or meaty. From my mother's perspective, the benefits were twofold: I had very little interest in the world of young love, and she didn't have to worry about dinner or dessert for a solid three months.

For the crêpes, place the flour, sugar, and salt in a blender with the eggs, milk, butter, and vanilla. Add ¾ cup water. Blitz for 15 to 20 seconds, or until well combined. Using a blender helps develop a little bit of gluten in the mixture, which makes your crêpes less likely to break when cooking. Place the crêpe batter in the fridge for 1 hour, or up to 2 days, to hydrate the flour and allow any bubbles to subside.

Heat an 8-inch nonstick frying pan over medium heat and give it a quick mist of cooking spray if your nonstick tends to be a little, well, sticky. Pour about ¼ cup of the batter into the center of the pan and give it a swirl to evenly coat. Cook for 30 to 45 seconds, flip, and cook for another 15 to 20 seconds. Remove the crêpe to a cutting board to cool, and continue to cook and stack crêpes until all of the batter is used up. Set the crêpes aside to cool while you make the filling.

For the filling, whip the cream and icing sugar to soft peaks using an electric mixer, about 1 to 2 minutes on medium speed. Add in the mascarpone cheese and whip to combine. In a small bowl, combine the marsala, vanilla, and espresso powder. Add this along with the salt to the cream mixture and continue to whip just until light and fluffy, about 2 to 3 minutes.

To build the cake, line the bottom and sides of an 8-inch springform pan with plastic wrap, leaving some hanging over the edge. Lay a crêpe on the bottom of the pan and spread a hefty ¼ cup of the cream filling on top in a thin, even layer. Repeat these layers until you are out of crêpes or filling, or you reach the top of the springform pan, making sure you end with a crêpe. Wrap the overhanging plastic over the top of the cake and place it in the fridge for at least 4 hours, or, preferably, overnight, to allow it to firm up.

When you're ready to serve, invert the pan onto a serving dish, release the sides, and remove the bottom. Peel off the plastic wrap and decorate with any additional filling, a dusting of cocoa, some fresh raspberries, and a little bit of icing sugar.

Note:

This is the ultimate make-ahead dish. The crêpes can be made several days ahead of assembly and stored in a resealable plastic bag in the fridge. The cake can be assembled and stored in the springform pan for up to 2 days before serving.

Hummingbird Cake, aka Breakfast Cake

MAKES 1 (9-INCH) THREE-LAYER CAKE

FOR THE CAKE

3 cups all-purpose flour
2 teaspoons baking soda
2 teaspoons baking powder
1 teaspoon fine salt
1 tablespoon ground cinnamon
¼ teaspoon freshly grated nutmeg
1 cup chopped pecans
3 eggs
2 cups granulated sugar
1 cup vegetable oil
2 teaspoons pure vanilla extract
2 cups roughly mashed ripe bananas (around 5 bananas)
1 cup crushed pineapple with its juice

FOR THE FROSTING

2 (each 8 oz) packages brick cream cheese
1 cup unsalted butter
4–6 cups icing sugar
2 teaspoons pure vanilla extract
½ teaspoon ground cinnamon
1 cup chopped pecans (optional)

When I was growing up, hummingbird cake was a staple in our house. Chock full of bananas, pecans, spices, and pineapple, it's pretty much a fruit version of carrot cake and easily sneaks into the realm of breakfast. Feel free to bake it as a layer cake, or go the more traditional breakfast route with a Bundt pan.

Preheat your oven to 350°F and grease three 9-inch round cake pans, lining the bottoms with parchment paper.

For the cake, in a large bowl, sift together the flour, baking soda, baking powder, salt, cinnamon, and nutmeg. Stir in the pecans and set aside. In the bowl of your stand mixer or with an electric mixer, cream the eggs with the sugar until the mixture is a lovely pale yellow, about 2 minutes. With the mixer running, stream in the oil and then the vanilla. Stir in the bananas and pineapple, including the juice. Add the dry ingredients to the wet and mix just until combined.

Divide the batter between the three cake pans and bake for 40 to 45 minutes, or until a toothpick inserted into the center of the cake comes out clean. Allow the cakes to cool for 10 minutes in their pans and then turn them out onto a wire rack to cool completely.

For the frosting, use either an electric mixer or a stand mixer fitted with a paddle attachment to beat the cream cheese and butter together until smooth. Begin adding the icing sugar, ½ cup at a time, mixing on low in between each addition and scraping down the sides of the bowl as needed. Keep adding icing sugar until your cream cheese frosting is a spreadable consistency. Finish it off by beating in the vanilla and cinnamon.

Decorate your cooled cakes however you see fit. Personally, I'm a fan of a cake with un-iced sides à la Christina Tosi, topped with extra pecans.

Note:

If you're going the Bundt pan route, just bake the cake at 350°F for 1 hour and 15 minutes, or until a toothpick inserted in the center of the cake comes out clean. Frost with a half batch of the cream cheese frosting or thin it out a bit with whipping cream to form a glaze. All of the ingredient measurements will still be correct—it's a magic cake!

Cocktail Parties

FOR AN INDECISIVE HOST

LEFT TO RIGHT:

SALTED PLUM NEGRONI SPRITZ (PAGE 70)

ARMAGNAC SIDECAR (PAGE 71)

VANILLA ORANGE CARDAMOM SPRITZ (PAGE 73)

TRUE CANADIAN COCKTAIL (PAGE 72)

Salted Plum Negroni Spritz

SERVES 8

Ice cubes, for stirring and serving
1 cup gin
1 cup Campari
1 cup sweet vermouth
1 cup sparkling wine
8 strips orange peel (see note)
8 salted plums
Cocktail picks

Salted plums are shrivelly, super-sour dried plums that can be found in Chinese markets and grocery stores. They give this Negroni spritz a great flavor, but if you can't find them, don't fret. A good maraschino cherry will do. The cocktail will taste slightly different, but it'll still be one heck of a delicious drink.

In a pitcher filled with about 2 cups of ice cubes, combine the gin, Campari, and sweet vermouth. Give it a good stir for about 30 seconds and then strain it into eight glasses with some fresh rocks. Add the sparkling wine and garnish with orange peel and a salted plum skewered on a cocktail pick.

Note:
To make a classic citrus peel cocktail garnish, use a vegetable peeler to remove a 1- to 2-inch strip of peel from a whole fruit, being careful not to take too much of the bitter white pith. Give the peel a twist just before using in a cocktail to release some of the oils from the zest.

Armagnac Sidecar

SERVES 8

- 1 lemon wedge
- ¼ cup granulated sugar
- 2 cups armagnac
- 1 cup orange liqueur
- 1 cup lemon juice (about 4 lemons)
- Ice cubes (optional)
- Maraschino cherries and lemon peel (see note on page 70), for garnish

The first time I ever had a Sidecar, one quickly turned into five . . . I was in New Orleans with my mom, hopping around jazz clubs along Frenchmen Street, and we ended up at this place that is somehow simultaneously a bar, dance hall, music venue, and bowling alley. It was amazing, but it ultimately led to my calling room service at 3:30 a.m. to order an overpriced grilled cheese sandwich. The moral of the story here is that Sidecars are delicious, but, as they are essentially a mix of tart citrus and rocket fuel, one or two should do.

Sugar the glasses by running the lemon wedge around the rim of your rocks glasses and evenly sprinkling the sugar on a small plate. Dip the rim of each glass into the sugar and set aside to dry.

In a large pitcher, stir together the armagnac, orange liqueur, and lemon juice, and then place it in the freezer for about 1 hour.

When you're ready to serve, give the mixture a good stir or shake. I prefer my cocktails to be quite punchy, but if you'd prefer, add some ice to your prepared glasses and pour the cocktail over top.

To garnish, place a few maraschino cherries and a piece of lemon peel onto a cocktail pin or toothpick and serve.

Note:
All the components of this cocktail can be prepared ahead of time. Sugar the glasses (or only sugar half the rim, if you're like me and prefer a tart cocktail), mix up the booze, prepare some garnish, and all you'll have to do is pour when cocktail hour strikes.

True Canadian Cocktail

SERVES 8

- 2 cups Canadian rye
- 1 cup sweet vermouth
- 10–15 dashes cherry or orange bitters
- ¼ cup pure maple syrup
- Ice cubes
- Frozen cranberries, cherries, or maple candies, for garnish

This cocktail is made in homage to my namesake and nana. She had quite the life, from winning Miss Canada in 1942 and 1943, to becoming the most popular lady at her retirement community down in Florida. While she would have ordered Canadian Club on the rocks with water on the side, this little number has a bit more style, which she had in spades.

In a large pitcher, combine the rye, sweet vermouth, bitters, and maple syrup and stir well. Serve in rocks glasses over ice with, in true Nana fashion, a cocktail napkin underneath. To get extra Canada points, garnish the drinks with cranberries, cherries, or maple candies.

Note:
Store any lingering mix in the fridge and give it a good stir before serving over ice.

Vanilla Orange Cardamom Spritz

SERVES 8–10

- ½ cup granulated sugar
- 1 vanilla bean, split and scraped
- 6–8 green cardamom pods, lightly crushed with the side of a knife
- Grated zest of 1 orange
- 1 cup orange juice
- 1 bottle prosecco or cava, chilled
- 1 orange, supremed (see note)

This drink is a combination of all of my favorite supporting flavors. In other recipes, these ingredients might not be noticed (even though they can make or break a dish), but here, these background actors get their chance to take center stage!

In a small pot set over medium-low heat, combine the sugar, vanilla bean pulp, cardamom pods, and orange zest with 1 cup of water. Simmer for 5 to 10 minutes, without stirring, to dissolve the sugar. Remove this vanilla cardamom syrup from the heat and allow the mixture to steep for 20 minutes. Strain and chill.

Mix the chilled syrup with orange juice and pour about ¼ cup of the mix into each glass. Top with prosecco and an orange supreme and serve.

Note:

To supreme an orange (or grapefruit), trim off the top and bottom of the fruit. Place the fruit on its end and, using a sharp knife, remove the peel and pith by slicing down along the curve of the fruit. Hold the fruit in your hand and carefully cut out each segment by inserting your knife between the flesh of the fruit and the membrane on both sides of each segment.

Cacio e Pepe Popcorn

SERVES 6–8, OR 1 MARY

- 2 tablespoons vegetable oil
- ½ cup popcorn kernels
- 3–4 tablespoons unsalted butter, melted
- ¾ cup finely grated Parmesan cheese
- ½ cup finely grated Pecorino Romano cheese
- 1 teaspoon fine sea salt
- 1 teaspoon freshly ground black pepper

Popcorn is my vice. I've been known to eat an entire extra-large bag during the previews prior to a movie, only to polish off another full bag by the time the credits roll around. Plain old popcorn is always great, but zhuzhing it up with the flavors of the snazziest, easiest cheesy pasta is never something I would turn my nose up at. This is the perfect addition to a cocktail party spread or just a night in on the couch with some Nora Ephron.

Heat a large stockpot with a tight-fitting lid over medium-high heat and set out a large mixing bowl. Once the pot is hot, add the oil and allow it to heat for about 1 minute. Stir in the popcorn kernels and cover with the lid.

Continuously shake the pot directly over the heat until the popping slows and it sounds like most of the kernels have popped. Immediately remove the pot from the heat and dump the popped corn into the large mixing bowl. Toss the melted butter onto the popcorn, followed by both cheeses, the salt, and pepper. Toss well to evenly distribute the toppings and serve.

Kettle Corn

SERVES 6–8

¼ cup vegetable oil
¼ cup granulated sugar
1 teaspoon fine sea salt
½ cup popcorn kernels

There is a pretty incriminating photo of my mother polishing off a bag of kettle corn the size of a large tree trunk. I'd probably never be forgiven if I shared it with anyone, but just picture her lounging in a recliner, looking simultaneously proud and ashamed of her accomplishment and you'll get the idea. The perfect combination of sweet and savory, this has Myra Berg's resounding seal of approval.

Heat a large stockpot with a tight-fitting lid over medium-high heat and line a large baking sheet with parchment paper. Once the pot is hot, add the oil and allow it to heat for about 1 minute. Stir in the sugar and salt, followed by the popcorn kernels. Give everything a stir and quickly cover with the lid.

Continuously shake the pot directly over the heat until the popping slows and it sounds like most of the kernels have popped. Immediately remove the pot from the heat and dump the kettle corn out onto the prepared baking sheet to cool completely.

Marinated Olives

MAKES 3 CUPS

3 cups mixed brine-cured olives
1 cup extra virgin olive oil
2 teaspoons dried chili flakes
1½ teaspoons cumin seeds
Grated zest and juice of 1 lemon
2 cloves garlic, thinly sliced
¼ teaspoon freshly ground black pepper

You know when you meet a new friend and something just clicks? That's what happened when I met perhaps the loudest, most feisty best friend a gal could ask for, Marisa Bruch. For months, every new thing I learned about her just made it more obvious that we were meant to be buds for life. That is, until I found out that she hates olives. To this day, I still don't understand. They're salty, earthy, fruity, dark, and amazing. I guess even soul mates have their differences . . .

In a large container or jar, combine the olives and olive oil. Lightly toast the chili flakes and cumin seeds in a small dry pan over medium heat until fragrant, about 1 minute. Add the toasted spices to the olives along with the lemon zest and juice, garlic, and pepper. Give the whole mixture a stir, pop on a lid, and allow it to marinate in the fridge for at least 2 days.

To serve, remove the olives from the fridge to allow them to come to room temperature or heat them gently in a pot over low heat for 1 to 2 minutes.

The olives can be stored in your fridge for up to 1 month.

Note:
These olives not only can, but should, be made well in advance. In terms of varieties, just choose your favorites. Personally, I'm partial to big, plump green olives and shriveled little black olives.

Smoked Mackerel Rillette

SERVES 10–12

- 4 hot-smoked mackerel fillets, deboned and skin removed (see note)
- ¾ cup brick-style cream cheese
- ½ cup sour cream
- 2 teaspoons smooth Dijon mustard
- 1 teaspoon grainy Dijon mustard
- 1½ teaspoons prepared horseradish
- 1 teaspoon grated lemon zest
- 2–3 tablespoons lemon juice
- 3 tablespoons finely chopped flat-leaf parsley, plus some for garnish
- Kosher salt
- Freshly ground black pepper
- ¼ cup salted butter, melted
- 1 baguette, sliced, or a few dozen crackers, for serving

Rillette is typically a super-heavy and fatty pork dish similar to pâté, but I thought that it was about time that I lightened up a classic rillette by replacing the pork and rendered fat with smoky mackerel and smooth cream cheese. Thinned a bit with sour cream and seasoned with mustard, horseradish, and lemon, this is one of my all-time favorite spreadables.

Place 3 of the deboned and skinned mackerel fillets in the bowl of your food processor fitted with a steel blade, followed by the cream cheese, sour cream, both Dijons, horseradish, lemon zest, and lemon juice. Give everything a good blitz until it is well combined and a spreadable consistency.

Transfer the mixture to a bowl and flake in the remaining mackerel fillet. Add in the parsley, season with salt and pepper, and stir to combine.

Scoop the rillette into two serving bowls or ramekins, smooth down the tops, and pour a thin layer of the butter over the rillettes—using a couple of serving dishes provides a good ratio of the cold butter to rillette filling but feel free to make just one large rillette if that's more your style. Scatter the extra parsley over top and place the rillettes in the fridge to set up.

Serve with lots of bread and crackers for spreading.

Note:

Smoked mackerel fillets can be found at your local fishmonger. If mackerel is not available, hot-smoked trout or salmon are perfect substitutes.

Roasted Tomatoes

SERVES 8–10

- 15–18 Roma tomatoes
- ¾ cup olive oil
- 1 tablespoon balsamic vinegar
- 1 teaspoon Italian seasoning
- 1 teaspoon kosher salt
- ¼ teaspoon freshly ground black pepper
- 3 cloves garlic, minced
- ½ cup finely chopped flat-leaf parsley
- 4½ oz soft goat cheese

I don't think I'd be lying if I said that I make these roasted tomatoes every single time I have people over or I'm headed to a friend's for dinner. Trying to think back, I cannot think of an instance that I didn't have these on hand—and with good reason. They are *so* good.

Preheat your oven to 350°F and prepare your tomatoes by quartering them and discarding the juicy pulp from the inside (save them for an ultra-tomato-y Caesar or Bloody Mary or simply add them to the compost pile).

Place the tomatoes in a glass or ceramic 9- × 13-inch baking dish along with the oil, balsamic, Italian seasoning, salt, and pepper.

Roast the tomatoes for 1 hour and 15 minutes, stirring every once in a while. As soon as you remove them from the oven, stir in the garlic and parsley and allow the tomatoes to cool slightly. Serve warm or at room temperature, with the goat cheese scattered over top.

White Bean Arugula Pizza Bianco

SERVES 8–12

- 2 tablespoons cornmeal
- 1 (1½ lb) ball store-bought pizza dough
- 2 cups ricotta cheese
- 1 cup grated Parmigiano-Reggiano cheese
- 2 cloves garlic, minced
- ¼ cup finely chopped flat-leaf parsley
- 1½ teaspoons chili flakes, divided
- 1 teaspoon kosher salt
- Grated zest and juice of 2 lemons, divided
- 1½ cups canned white kidney beans, rinsed and drained
- 4 tablespoons olive oil, divided
- Kosher salt
- Freshly ground black pepper
- 3–4 cups shredded mozzarella cheese
- 5–6 cups lightly packed arugula
- 3½–4½ oz thinly sliced prosciutto
- 1 oz shaved Parmigiano-Reggiano cheese
- Balsamic reduction (see page 81)

White beans are one of the many edible canvases often hidden in the back of our pantries. Dressed with a little olive oil, some lemon juice, and a bit of chili, they absorb and enhance the flavors of this hearty and delicious pizza bianca.

Preheat your oven to 450°F, set out two baking sheets, and dust each one with 1 tablespoon of cornmeal. Remove the pizza dough from the fridge and allow it to come to room temperature while you prepare the toppings.

In a bowl, stir together both cheeses, the garlic, parsley, ½ teaspoon of the chili flakes, and the salt with the zest and juice of 1 lemon. In a separate bowl, combine the remaining chili flakes, and the zest and juice of the remaining lemon with the kidney beans and 2 tablespoons of the olive oil. Season with a bit of salt and pepper and, using a fork, smash it all up a bit.

Separate your pizza dough into two equal pieces, then stretch each one into a long, thin oval and place it on a baking sheet. Top each base with half of the ricotta mixture followed by the mozzarella. Bake the pizzas for 18 to 22 minutes, or until the cheese is golden and the crust is crisp.

Meanwhile, toss the arugula with the remaining 2 tablespoons of olive oil and season with a pinch of salt and pepper.

Remove the pizzas from the oven, transfer them to a serving platter or board, and allow to cool slightly. Scatter the tops with the white bean mixture, followed by the dressed arugula, thinly sliced prosciutto, shaved Parmigiano-Reggiano, and a drizzle of balsamic reduction. Cut the pizzas into strips and serve still hot from the oven or at room temperature.

Balsamic Reduction

MAKES ¼ CUP

½ cup balsamic vinegar
¼ teaspoon kosher salt
Freshly cracked black pepper

In a small pot, simmer the balsamic over medium heat until reduced by half, about 8 to 12 minutes. Season with the salt and pepper and allow to cool. Use immediately or store in the fridge for up to 1 year in a tightly sealed container.

ricotta
grape
hazelnut
Pea
Prosciutto
Blue
Butternut
Walnut
Plum
Honey
Goat
grilled
corn
Pancetta
Brie
Cress

Tartine Bar

PICK THREE COMBINATIONS TO SERVE 8–10

The only thing that is mandatory for your tartine bar is a whole whack of thinly sliced fresh bread and little golden toasts. To make the toasts, just thinly slice a baguette or two, lay the slices out on a large sheet pan, and give them a drizzle of olive oil and a sprinkling of salt and pepper. Pop them into a 400°F oven for 15 to 20 minutes, flipping halfway through. Set your fresh bread and toast out on a big wooden board, make a flavor palate out of as many topping combinations as you'd like, and let your guests do the rest of the work.

Pancetta, Oozy Brie, and Cress

1½–2½ oz thinly sliced pancetta
1 large handful watercress, torn
2 teaspoons olive oil
1 teaspoon balsamic vinegar
Kosher salt
Freshly ground black pepper
1 small wheel or wedge of Brie cheese

Cook the pancetta in a large frying pan over medium heat until crisp, about 1 to 2 minutes per side, and then allow to cool to room temperature.

Meanwhile, toss the watercress with the oil and balsamic and season with a little salt and pepper.

Set the pancetta, watercress, and Brie out onto your board for tartine building. To assemble, simply stack all of this goodness onto a toast or slice of bread.

Blue Cheese, Butternut Squash, and Walnuts

- ½ small butternut squash, seeds removed
- 2 tablespoons olive oil, divided
- 1 tablespoon pure maple syrup
- 1 teaspoon finely chopped fresh sage
- ¼ teaspoon freshly grated nutmeg
- Kosher salt
- Freshly ground black pepper
- 4½–5 oz blue cheese
- ¾ cup toasted whole walnuts

Preheat your oven to 400°F and line a baking sheet with aluminum foil. Brush the flesh side of the butternut squash with about 1 teaspoon of the oil and place it, flesh side down, on the prepared baking sheet. Bake the squash for 35 to 45 minutes, or until tender, and then allow it to cool to room temperature.

When it's cool, scoop out all the flesh and mash it up in a bowl with the remaining oil, the maple syrup, sage, nutmeg, and a bit of salt and pepper. Set the bowl on your tartine board along with the blue cheese and toasted walnuts.

To assemble, place a good dollop of the squash onto a slice of bread, followed by some blue cheese and a few walnuts.

Grilled Corn, Avocado, and Cotija Cheese

- 2 ears corn, shucked
- ¼ cup good-quality mayonnaise
- ¼ cup sour cream
- ½ teaspoon garlic powder
- ½ teaspoon chili powder
- 3 tablespoons lime juice, divided (about 2 limes)
- 2½–3½ oz crumbled Cotija cheese (see note)
- 1 avocado, diced
- 2 tablespoons finely chopped cilantro
- ¼ teaspoon cayenne pepper

Preheat your grill or grill pan to medium-high heat and grill the corn, turning occasionally, for 7 to 10 minutes, or until it's nicely charred on all sides. Set the corn aside to cool to room temperature.

Meanwhile, in a small bowl, combine the mayonnaise, sour cream, garlic powder, chili powder, and 2 tablespoons of the lime juice. Set aside.

When the corn is cool, use a knife to cut off all the kernels. Place the kernels in a bowl and add in the remaining lime juice, the cheese, avocado, cilantro, and cayenne pepper.

To assemble, spread some of the mayonnaise mixture onto a piece of bread and top with a good spoonful of the corn salsa.

Note:

If you can't find Cotija cheese, feta is a good substitute.

Plum and Honeyed Goat Cheese

- 1 tablespoon olive oil
- 4–5 red plums, stones removed and sliced
- 1 teaspoon dried thyme, divided
- Kosher salt
- Freshly ground black pepper
- 4½ oz soft goat cheese
- 2 tablespoons liquid honey

Place a large frying pan over medium heat. When it's hot, add the oil followed by the plum slices. Stir in ½ teaspoon of the thyme and season the plums with salt and pepper. Allow the plums to cook, stirring frequently, for about 4 to 6 minutes, or until they are soft and a little jammy.

Meanwhile, mix the remaining ½ teaspoon of thyme with the goat cheese and honey, and season with a bit of salt and pepper.

When the plums are done, transfer them to a serving dish and place them on your tartine board.

To assemble, spread a good amount of the honeyed goat cheese onto some bread and top with a dollop of the plums.

Minty Green Pea Purée and Prosciutto

- 1 cup frozen peas, thawed
- 1 clove garlic, minced
- 2 tablespoons finely chopped fresh mint leaves
- Grated zest and juice of ½ lemon
- ½ teaspoon kosher salt
- ¼ teaspoon freshly ground black pepper
- ¼ cup unsalted butter, melted
- 4½–5 oz thinly sliced prosciutto

Using a food processor fitted with the steel blade or an immersion blender, purée the peas, garlic, mint, lemon zest and juice, salt, pepper, and melted butter until chunky or smooth, depending on how you like it.

To assemble, schmear the pea purée over a slice of toast and top with a piece of prosciutto.

Ricotta, Roasted Grapes, and Hazelnuts

2 cups seedless red grapes
2 tablespoons olive oil
Kosher salt
Freshly ground black pepper
3 tablespoons marsala wine or port
½ cup toasted hazelnuts, chopped
1 cup ricotta cheese
2 teaspoons lemon juice
½ teaspoon grated lemon zest

Preheat your oven to 450°F.

Toss the grapes with the olive oil and season them with a bit of salt and pepper. Roast them on a baking sheet for about 15 to 20 minutes or until they're a little blistered, shrivelly, and on the verge of bursting. Remove the grapes from the oven, transfer them to a frying pan, and set them over medium heat. When the pan is hot, remove it from the heat and carefully deglaze the pan with the marsala (or port). Stir in the hazelnuts and transfer the grapes to a small dish and allow them to cool.

Meanwhile, mix together the ricotta and lemon juice and zest in a small bowl and season with salt and pepper.

To assemble, slather some toasts with ricotta and top with the grapes and hazelnuts.

Note:

If you're looking for a bit of a show, try flambéing the grapes. After adding the marsala or port, carefully tilt the pan over the flame of your stove to ignite the alcohol's vapors. If you're not cooking over gas, you can lightly and quickly hover a long wooden fireplace match over the edge of the alcohol. Either way, be careful! Nothing ruins a party like an eyebrowless host.

Ol' Cheddar onion

Mozz Raspberry Basil

Gruyère Mustard

Blackberry Blue

Pecorino Honey

There's No Such Thing as Too Much Cheese . . .

Okay, okay, this is less a recipe and more a rambling list of all of the things I do to really snazz up my cheese board, because, in my opinion, a party isn't a party unless there is too much cheese. Here are my Berg-approved cheese board zhuzhables:

Pecorino and Honey

Place a wedge of Pecorino Romano on your board and give it a drizzle with some runny honey or, better yet, drape a piece of honeycomb on there. Finish the cheese off with a sprinkling of freshly ground black pepper and you're golden.

Mozzarella, Raspberries, and Basil

It's all in the name. Just tear up a big ball of fresh mozzarella cheese and smash some raspberries on top. Give the whole mess a drizzle with some good extra virgin olive oil, a scattering of torn-up basil leaves, and a pinch of coarse salt.

Extra-Old Cheddar with Caramelized Onions

This one involves a little bit of work. For the caramelized onions, thinly slice 2 yellow onions and place them in a medium-sized frying pan with 1 tablespoon of olive oil. Season with salt and pepper and slowly cook the onions over medium-low heat for 30 minutes, stirring occasionally. Drizzle in 1 tablespoon of pure maple syrup and cook for another 10 minutes or so, or until the onions are deeply caramelized. To serve, break up a hunk of extra-old white cheddar cheese and spoon the onions over top.

Gruyère with Snazzed-Up Mustard

Combine a few tablespoons of your favorite Dijon mustard with a glug of good-quality extra virgin olive oil, a few grinds of pepper, and a scattering of herbes de Provence. Paired with Gruyère and some crusty baguette, this just feels like the beginnings of something very French to me.

Blue Cheese and Blackberry Rosemary Freezer Jam

See page 44 for my super-quick and easy Blackberry Rosemary Freezer Jam. Pair that with a big old hunk of stinky blue cheese and, boy oh boy, love is in the air.

Jammy Baked Fontina

SERVES 6–8

- ½ cup mixed berry jam
- 10½–12½ oz diced fontina cheese, rind removed
- 2 tablespoons olive oil
- ½ teaspoon kosher salt
- ½ teaspoon freshly ground black pepper
- 2 tablespoons finely chopped fresh basil
- 1 baguette

Jam always makes its way onto my cheese boards, so I figured why not just join the two together in melty matrimony? Stringy, golden, and fruity, this baked fontina goes fast, so make sure you sneak a few bites before you bring it out to your guests.

Position an oven rack in the center of the oven and preheat the broiler.

Spread the jam in an even layer across the bottom of a small cast iron skillet or a 6- to 8-inch heatproof serving dish and scatter the cheese over top. Drizzle it with the oil and season with the salt and pepper.

Place the skillet (or dish) under the broiler for 4 to 6 minutes, or until the cheese is bubbling and golden brown. Serve the cheese in the skillet, garnished with a scattering of fresh basil alongside big chunks of baguette.

Note:
Once the fontina has cooled, it will no longer be stringy, so use a spoon or cheese knife to serve this.

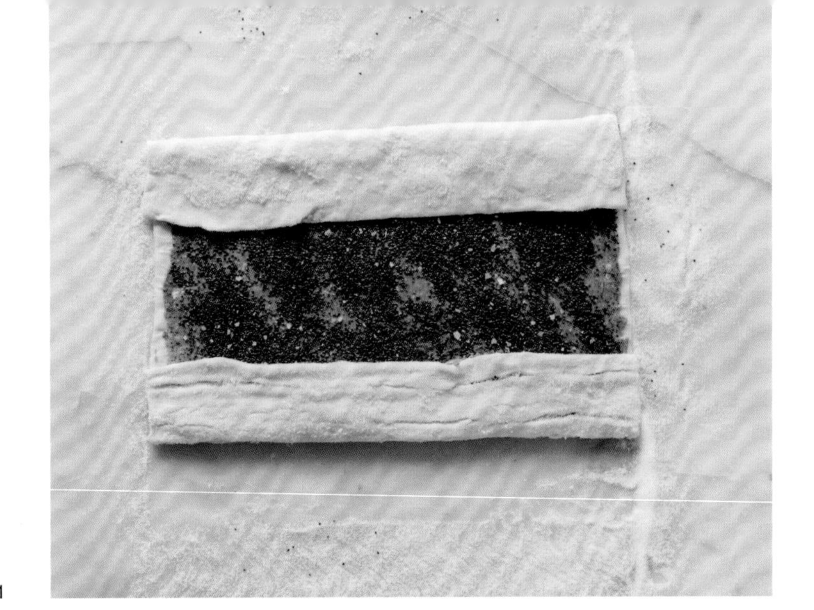

1

2

3

Poppy Seed Almond Butter Palmiers

MAKES 30 PALMIERS

- 2 tablespoons granulated sugar
- 1 sheet of frozen puff pastry, thawed
- ⅓ cup unsweetened almond butter
- 1½ tablespoons poppy seeds
- ¼ teaspoon kosher salt

Perhaps the world's simplest cookies, what with store-bought puff pastry being so readily available, these palmiers lean toward the savory side with their almond butter and poppy seed filling, and pair beautifully with cocktails. The best part? This recipe makes enough for you to snack on any less-than-perfect ones before your guests arrive.

Line two baking sheets with parchment paper.

Sprinkle the sugar over a clean work surface and unroll the thawed puff pastry on top. Very lightly press the pastry down onto the sugar so that some sticks to the underside. Thinly spread the almond butter on top of the pastry, making sure to cover every inch, then evenly sprinkle the poppy seeds and salt over top.

To form the palmiers, fold the two sides of the pastry halfway to the center (see fig. 1) and then again so the sides meet in the middle (fig. 2). Fold one half over the other, like you're closing a greeting card, and place the whole roll onto one of the prepared baking sheets.

Preheat your oven to 450°F.

Place the roll in the freezer for 10 to 15 minutes to firm up, then cut it into ¼-inch slices with a very sharp knife (fig. 3). Lay the slices on the prepared baking sheets and bake for 7 to 9 minutes, or until golden brown on the bottom. Flip the palmiers over and bake for an additional 3 to 4 minutes, or until golden brown and delicious all around.

Cool the palmiers on a wire rack and serve alongside cocktails or a cup of tea.

Note:

You can store the palmiers in an airtight container for up to 5 days.

LEFT: PALMIERS (PAGE 93)

RIGHT: FRITTERS (PAGE 96)

Raspberry Cardamom Fritters

SERVES 8–10

- Vegetable oil, for deep frying
- 1 cup all-purpose flour
- ¼ cup granulated sugar
- 1½ teaspoons baking powder
- 1 teaspoon ground cardamom
- ¼ teaspoon fine sea salt
- ⅛ teaspoon freshly grated nutmeg
- 1 egg
- ¼ cup + 2 tablespoons buttermilk
- 1 tablespoon melted unsalted butter
- 1 teaspoon pure vanilla extract
- ½ cup fresh raspberries
- Icing sugar or cardamom orange glaze (see page 97)

Pretty much every Saturday morning during my undergrad years, I would drag at least one of my roommates out of bed at an unearthly hour to join me on my weekly trek to the farmers' market. We would wait in a line that stretched around the building for freshly made, piping-hot apple fritters. I've since figured out an easier way to get my fritter fix. I make glorious homemade fritters of any kind whenever the notion strikes, and my roommate (read: husband) gets a good sleep in on Saturday mornings—what could be better?

Heat about 3 inches of vegetable oil in a large, deep pot over medium heat until a kitchen thermometer registers 340°F or bubbles form around a wooden spoon that has been submerged. Set a wire rack over a baking sheet.

Meanwhile, sift the flour, sugar, baking powder, cardamom, salt, and nutmeg into a large bowl. In a separate bowl, whisk together the egg, buttermilk, butter, and vanilla. Add the wet ingredients to the dry, stir until almost combined, and then gently fold in the raspberries.

When the oil is at temperature, use a large tablespoon or small ice cream scoop to carefully drop five or six spoonfuls of batter into the hot oil. Fry the fritters until golden brown all around, about 2 to 3 minutes per side.

Remove the fritters from the oil and place them on the prepared wire rack to drain and cool slightly. Continue until you've used all of the batter and you have about 16 to 20 fritters.

To dress the fritters up a bit, allow them to cool slightly, then dust them with a good helping of icing sugar before serving, or drizzle or dunk into cardamom orange glaze.

Cardamom Orange Glaze

1 cup icing sugar
½ teaspoon ground cardamom
3–5 tablespoons freshly squeezed orange juice
1 tablespoon unsalted butter, melted
1 teaspoon grated orange zest

In a small bowl, whisk the icing sugar and ground cardamom with 3 tablespoons of the orange juice, the butter and orange zest. If the glaze is not thin enough to evenly and lightly coat the back of a spoon, whisk in a little more orange juice, about 1 teaspoon at a time, until it is the right consistency. Dunk your slightly cooled fritters into the glaze, making sure you coat every single inch, and allow them to dry completely on a wire rack set over a baking sheet. You can also drizzle the glaze over the fritters for a not-so-sweet option.

Brown Butter Coconut Financiers

MAKES 15 FINANCIERS

- ¾ cup unsalted butter
- ½ cup granulated sugar
- ¼ cup brown sugar, packed
- ½ cup all-purpose flour
- ¼ cup + 2 tablespoons almond flour, plus more for sprinkling
- ¼ cup finely ground unsweetened coconut (see note)
- 1½ teaspoons baking powder
- 1 teaspoon kosher salt
- Zest of 1 lemon
- 5 egg whites
- 1 teaspoon pure vanilla extract

My husband calls these "Fancy Guys" which I think, ironically, makes him not a very fancy guy . . . The perfect balance of sweet, salty, and nutty, these chewy and crisp financiers combine so many good flavors into just a few bites.

In a small pot, cook the butter over medium heat, stirring frequently until dark and golden but not burnt, about 4 to 6 minutes. Keep a close eye on it, as the butter can burn fairly quickly. Once the butter is browned, transfer it to a heatproof bowl, being sure to scrape out all of the brown butter bits from the bottom of the pot.

Combine both sugars, both flours, the coconut, baking powder, salt, and lemon zest in a medium bowl. Add the hot browned butter to the dry mixture and quickly beat to incorporate. Set the batter aside for about 5 minutes to allow it to cool slightly, and then mix in the egg whites and vanilla. Cover the bowl with plastic wrap and chill in the fridge for at least 1 hour, or up to 24 hours.

When you're ready to bake, preheat the oven to 375°F and lightly grease a silicone financier pan or one 12-cup muffin tin, plus 3 additional cups in a second tin, with cooking spray. Sprinkle the pan(s) lightly with a little more almond flour and shake to coat. Divide the batter evenly between the cups of the prepared pan and bake for 20 to 25 minutes or until golden and springy.

Allow the financiers to sit in the pan for about 5 minutes, then turn them out onto a wire rack to cool completely before serving.

Note:

Dried coconut comes in many sizes, from flaked to shredded to ground. You'll want to use the finest ground coconut possible.

Dinner Parties

FOR LEISURELY DINERS

No-Knead Bread and Homemade Butter

MAKES 1 LOAF AND ABOUT 3/4 CUP OF BUTTER

FOR THE BREAD

1 3/4–2 cups white bread flour
1 cup whole wheat flour
2 1/2 teaspoons instant/rapid-rise yeast
1 1/2 teaspoons kosher salt
1 1/2 cups warm water
2 teaspoons liquid honey

FOR THE BUTTER

2 cups whipping (35%) cream
1/4–1/2 teaspoon fine sea salt, depending on how salty you like your butter
Cheesecloth

Yeah, you read that right.

Homemade.

Butter.

The ultimate in kitchen wizardry and, in true Mary fashion, way easier than it seems.

For the bread, combine 1 3/4 cups of the bread flour with the whole wheat flour, yeast, and salt in a large bowl and make a well in the center. In a separate bowl, whisk together the warm water and honey until the honey dissolves, then pour the mixture into the well. Using a wooden spoon, mix vigorously until a wet dough forms. Continue to mix vigorously for 2 to 3 minutes to develop the gluten, adding more bread flour, 1/4 cup at a time, if needed, until the dough comes together. Cover the bowl with plastic wrap and a clean kitchen towel and place the dough in a warm place to rise for about 1 hour or until doubled in size.

Meanwhile, place a Dutch oven with its lid in a cold oven and preheat the oven to 450°F. When the oven is at temperature and the dough has risen, generously flour a work surface and gently tip the dough out onto it, using a spatula to help it release from the bowl. Gently fold the edges of the dough into the center to help shape the dough into a rough round. Flip the loaf over so that it is seam side down.

Carefully transfer the Dutch oven to the stovetop or a heatproof surface. Place a few tablespoons of water in a bowl set beside the Dutch oven. Remove the lid from the hot Dutch oven and carefully drop the dough in. Don't worry if the loaf loses its shape at this point—I promise it will look great after it's baked. Using a paring knife, slice a little slit in the top of the loaf. Flick a splash of water on the underside of the hot lid and quickly put the lid back on the Dutch oven. Return the Dutch oven to the oven to bake the bread for 15 minutes. Remove the lid and bake for another 30 minutes, then place the bread on a wire rack to cool.

For the butter, place the cream in a food processor fitted with a steel blade and blitz on high for about 5 minutes. When the sound changes, it's a sign that the butter fat has separated from the buttermilk. It looks kind of gross and curdled, but this is what you're aiming for! Strain the mixture through a fine mesh sieve lined with four layers of cheesecloth and give the mixture remaining in the sieve a gentle squeeze to remove as much of the buttermilk as possible. Transfer the butter to a bowl and mix in the salt. Wrap the butter in wax paper or parchment paper and serve at room temperature or chilled.

Note:
The buttermilk resulting from churning your own butter is thinner and less tangy than commercial buttermilks, but it's delicious used in pancake batter or poured over Baked Steel Cut Oatmeal (see page 51).

Summery Corn Soup

SERVES 6–8

- 3 tablespoons unsalted butter
- 1 cup finely diced shallots
- Kosher salt
- Freshly ground black pepper
- 8 ears corn, kernels removed and cobs reserved
- 4 cups vegetable broth
- 1 cup milk or half and half
- Fresh chives, for garnish

As late summer approaches, the scenery on the drive north to the cottage becomes scattered with corn stands, boasting a dozen ears for just a few bucks. Every year I tell myself that I'll stop in at one, but as soon as I hit the road, the only thing on my mind is hopping in the lake. After an initial swim, I'll usually boat over to our local blueberry lady, who always also has a few dozen ears for sale. It's fantastic straight off the cob, but this soup really brings it to life.

In a large stockpot, melt the butter over medium heat. Add the shallots, season with a bit of salt and pepper, and allow them to sweat for 3 to 4 minutes, or until tender.

Add in the corn kernels and cobs and the broth and bring the soup to a boil. Turn down the heat to low and simmer the soup, uncovered, for 15 to 20 minutes. Remove the cobs from the pot, pour in the milk (or cream), and blend with an immersion blender until the soup is very smooth. Give it a taste, season with a little more salt and pepper, and cover the pot with a tight-fitting lid.

Keep the soup warm over low heat until you're ready to serve. Garnish each serving with fresh chives. You could also serve this soup cold with a dollop of sour cream.

Note:
For a fancier garnish that's pretty darn simple to make, blend ¼ cup of extra virgin olive oil with 3 tablespoons of finely chopped chives and 1 tablespoon of finely chopped flat-leaf parsley until well combined. Drizzle this herby oil over the soup, storing any leftovers in the fridge for up to 1 week.

Fennel, Citrus, and Burrata Salad

SERVES 8

- 2 fennel bulbs, including fronds
- 2 yellow zucchinis
- 1 green zucchini
- 3 oranges, supremed (see page 73) + 2 tablespoons of reserved juice
- 2 grapefruits, supremed (see page 73) + 2 tablespoons of reserved juice
- ½ cup fresh mint, roughly chopped or torn
- ½ cup flat-leaf parsley, roughly chopped or torn
- ¼ cup olive oil
- 1 clove garlic, finely minced
- Kosher salt
- Freshly cracked black pepper
- 1 ball burrata
- Balsamic reduction (see page 81)

There are few things that go together as well as fennel and citrus. The licorice-y bite of that fantastically fronded bulb meets its perfect match in the sweetness of an orange. This recipe plays off the fennel/orange affair and brings in some supporting characters in the form of grapefruit, mint, zucchini, and a syrupy balsamic reduction. The brightness of these flavors makes it a perfect start to any meal.

Trim the bottom and top of the fennel, reserving the fronds for later use, quarter the bulbs, and remove most of the tough core. Using a mandoline or a vegetable peeler, very thinly slice the fennel and zucchinis and toss them in a large bowl along with the orange and grapefruit supremes. Add in the mint and parsley and set aside.

In a small bowl, whisk together the reserved orange and grapefruit juices, the oil, and garlic. Season with salt and pepper, pour the dressing over top, and gently toss everything together.

To plate, place your salad on a platter and top with the burrata ball. Carefully tear it open to allow its creamy insides to ooze out a little. Drizzle the salad with balsamic reduction and an extra glug of olive oil and finish with a bit more salt and pepper.

Note:
All of the citrus, vegetables, and herbs can be prepped up to 1 day in advance. Fresh mozzarella or feta will work wonderfully if you can't find burrata.

Sweet Pea and Asparagus Soup with Lemony Crème Fraîche

SERVES 8–10

FOR THE CRÈME FRAÎCHE

½ cup whipping (35%) cream
1 tablespoon buttermilk
Grated zest and juice of ½ lemon
Kosher salt

FOR THE SOUP

2 tablespoons unsalted butter
3 cloves garlic, minced
2 medium shallots, finely diced
1 large bundle asparagus, ends trimmed and stalks cut into 1-inch pieces
Kosher salt
Freshly ground black pepper
3 cups green peas, fresh or frozen and thawed
3–4 cups no- or low-sodium vegetable broth
½ cup finely chopped flat-leaf parsley, plus more for garnish
3–4 tablespoons finely chopped fresh mint, plus more for garnish
2 teaspoons grated lemon zest
½ cup milk or table (18%) cream
2 teaspoons lemon juice (optional)

I love those first weeks of outdoor farmers' markets in the spring. When I'm meandering around the stalls, the vivid greens and purples of fresh peas and asparagus always catch my eye. When they're quickly cooked into this bright green soup and paired with lemony crème fraîche, this is all I want to eat from April to June.

For the crème fraîche, combine the whipping cream and buttermilk in a small jar with a tight-fitting lid and give it a shake. Leave the jar out on the counter for 8 to 24 hours to thicken. I know that this sounds a little strange, but don't worry, you'll have delicious crème fraîche in no time.

Once it's thick, add in the lemon zest and juice and season with a pinch of salt. Reseal the jar and place it in the fridge to chill. Once chilled, the crème fraîche can be used right away or stored in the fridge, tightly sealed, for up to 1 week.

For the soup, place a large pot or stockpot over medium heat. Melt the butter and cook the garlic and shallots just until softened, about 2 to 3 minutes. Add in the asparagus, season with salt and pepper, and continue to cook for about 1 minute. Toss in the peas, followed by 3 cups of the broth, and bring the mixture to a boil. Turn down the heat to a simmer and cook just until the peas and asparagus are tender, about 3 to 4 minutes. Add in the parsley, mint, zest, and milk (or cream) and pour the whole lot into a blender (you might have to do this in batches) and blend on high. To save on dishes, use an immersion blender to blitz up the soup. The result will not be as silky smooth but it will still taste delicious. Give it a taste, and season with salt, pepper, and a squirt of lemon juice (if using). If the soup seems a little thick, thin it out with the remaining broth.

Serve hot or chilled, topped with a dollop of lemony crème fraîche and a scattering of mint and parsley.

Note:
If making crème fraîche doesn't seem like something you'd be interested in, feel free to season some store-bought crème fraîche or sour cream with lemon and a pinch of salt, to taste.

Oysters with Apple Jalapeño Mignonette

SERVES 8–12

½ cup apple cider vinegar
¼ cup green apple, peeled and very finely diced
1 tablespoon very finely diced jalapeño pepper
1 tablespoon very finely diced shallot
¼ teaspoon kosher salt
2 dozen freshly shucked oysters
Crushed ice
Jalapeño hot sauce, for serving

You always remember your first oyster. Good or bad, horribly or expertly shucked, there is always a story behind it. Classic mignonette is great, but if you're looking for a change, the sweet/sour/spicy flavor of this apple jalapeño mignonette is a game-changer.

In a small nonreactive bowl (i.e., glass or ceramic—not metal), combine the vinegar, apple, jalapeño, shallots, and salt. Allow this mignonette to sit and meld at room temperature for at least 10 minutes. Serve alongside oysters nestled on ice and some jalapeño hot sauce.

Salmon Tartare

SERVES 8

- 21 oz sushi-grade salmon, skin removed
- 3 tablespoons very finely chopped shallot
- 3 tablespoons red wine vinegar
- 3 tablespoons finely chopped fresh dill
- 2 tablespoons finely chopped fresh chives
- 2 tablespoons finely chopped flat-leaf parsley
- 2 tablespoons finely chopped capers
- 4 tablespoons lemon juice, divided
- 3 tablespoons extra virgin olive oil
- 2 tablespoons grainy Dijon mustard
- 2 teaspoons smooth Dijon mustard
- 1 teaspoon kosher salt, divided
- ¼ teaspoon freshly ground black pepper
- 1 bag salted kettle cooked potato chips, for serving

I could eat a bathtub's worth of salmon tartare. And that's kind of what I did while Aaron and I were in Paris for our honeymoon. At every restaurant we stopped at during our lengthy city walks, if salmon tartare was on the menu, I would immediately place an order for it along with a bottle of wine. This dish shouldn't be reserved for a honeymoon, though; it's equally delicious for a weeknight dinner at home. It's best served with salty, crunchy kettle cooked potato chips because . . . well, why not?

Before you begin, set your mixing bowl in a larger mixing bowl filled with ice. This will ensure that your tartare stays nice and chilled while you work.

Cut the salmon into ½-inch cubes and place them in the chilled mixing bowl.

In a separate small bowl, combine the shallots and vinegar and allow them to lightly pickle for 5 to 7 minutes while you prepare the rest of your ingredients.

Mix the dill, chives, parsley, and capers into the salmon. Drain and discard the vinegar from the shallots and add them to the salmon as well. Stir in 2 tablespoons of the lemon juice, the oil, both mustards, ½ teaspoon of the salt, and the pepper, and place the mixture in the fridge for 1 hour.

When you're ready to serve, transfer the salmon to a serving dish and season with the remaining lemon juice and salt. Serve with the kettle cooked potato chips and a bottle of your favorite French wine.

Steelhead Trout Gravlax

SERVES 8–10

½ cup kosher salt
½ cup brown sugar, packed
2 lb sushi-grade steelhead trout fillet, skin on, pin bones removed (see note)
3 sprigs tarragon
1 large bunch dill
1 (1-inch) piece fresh horseradish, peeled and finely grated
Grated zest of 1 lemon
1 tablespoon coarsely ground black pepper
Prepared horseradish, grainy Dijon mustard, lemon wedges, sour cream and/or cream cheese, capers, red onion, dill, and bready things, for serving

If you like cold-smoked salmon, you should give gravlax a try. It's like the freshly cured cousin of that breakfast-y, appetizer-y staple, and you won't set off your smoke alarm making it. It takes a few days to cure but minimal time and effort to prepare and serve, making it the perfect get-ahead party dish.

In a small bowl, mix together the salt and sugar. Rinse and thoroughly dry the trout and set it aside.

Line a large, deep dish, just big enough to hold the fish, with plastic wrap, allowing it to hang over the edges. Sprinkle one-third of the salt and sugar mixture into the bottom of the dish, making sure it's piled in a shape that sort of resembles the fillet. Lay one-third of the tarragon and dill on top of the salt and sugar, followed by the trout fillet, skin side down.

Scatter the grated horseradish and zest evenly over the flesh of the trout, followed by the remaining tarragon and dill, and the pepper. Sprinkle the fillet with the remaining sugar-salt mixture and bring the plastic wrap over the top to tightly wrap the fish. Place another piece of plastic wrap over the fish, followed by a slightly smaller dish weighted down with a few heavy cans.

Place the fish in the fridge to cure for a minimum of 2 days, or up to 3 days. After curing, it should be quite firm to the touch.

When you're ready to serve, unwrap the fish and give it a rinse under cold water to remove the cure. Lay the fillet out on a cutting board. Use a long, thin carving knife to slice off long thin strips, just like you would with cold-smoked salmon.

Serve with prepared horseradish, grainy Dijon, lemon wedges, sour cream and/or cream cheese, capers, red onion, dill, and lots of bagels, pumpernickel bread, or crackers.

Note:
Ask your fishmonger to remove the pin bones, as they can be tricky to remove with tweezers at home.

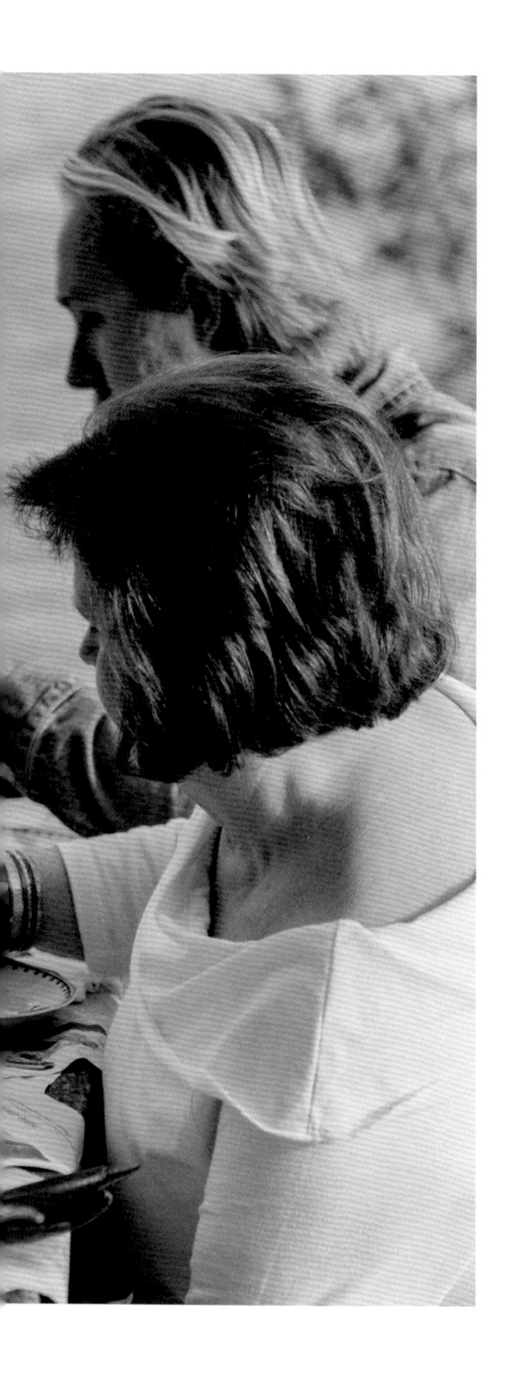

Bite-Sized Seafood Boil

SERVES 8

- 1 bottle crisp white wine, such as pinot grigio
- 2 lemons, halved
- 8 cloves garlic
- 1 yellow onion, peeled and quartered
- 1 rib celery, cut into large chunks
- ¼ cup Old Bay Seasoning
- 2 tablespoons kosher salt
- 2 bay leaves
- 2.2 lb mini potatoes
- 1 lb andouille sausage or kielbasa, cut into bite-sized pieces
- 24 littleneck clams, soaked, picked over, scrubbed and de-bearded
- 4 ears corn, shucked and halved
- 24–30 large unpeeled shrimp
- ½ cup unsalted butter
- 1 tablespoon liquid honey
- 1 teaspoon Cajun seasoning
- ½ teaspoon fine salt
- 4 lemons, quartered
- Tabasco sauce

Nothing says summer quite like a seafood boil served outside, scattered across yesterday's news. Just make sure you have lots of beer, white wine, and napkins on hand.

In a large stockpot filled with about 1 gallon of water, combine the white wine, halved lemons, garlic, onion, celery, Old Bay Seasoning, salt, and bay leaves.

Place the mini potatoes in the pot and bring to a boil over high heat. Once they're boiling, let them cook just until fork-tender, 5 to 10 minutes, depending on their size. Add in the sausage and cook for 5 more minutes. Next, add the scrubbed clams and corn and cook for 5 minutes. Finally, toss in the shrimp and cook for 3 minutes, or just until the clams are all open and the shrimp are pink. Discard any clams that do not open.

Meanwhile, mash together the butter, honey, Cajun seasoning, and salt in a small bowl and set aside.

Drain the seafood boil through a large colander and return to the pot or arrange on a large serving dish.

Serve immediately with the Cajun compound butter, lemon quarters, and lots of Tabasco sauce.

Flank Steak with Horseradish Cream

SERVES 8

- 1 (3½–4 lb) flank steak (see note)
- 1 tablespoon kosher salt
- 2 cups lager or another mild beer
- ½ cup olive oil
- ¼ cup + 2 tablespoons prepared horseradish, divided
- ¼ cup balsamic vinegar
- ¼ cup smooth Dijon mustard
- 1 large cooking onion, peeled and roughly chopped
- 8 cloves garlic, smashed and roughly chopped
- 2 teaspoons whole peppercorns
- 1 cup roughly torn flat-leaf parsley, stems and all
- 10 sprigs thyme
- 4 sprigs rosemary
- 1 cup sour cream
- 2 teaspoons Montreal steak spice

If you have the option, preparing one big piece of meat is always preferable when you're cooking for a crowd. This is a trick that I learned from none other than my mother, Myra Mama B, the queen of flank steaks. Rather than having eight pieces of meat of varying thickness sitting around your grill, you have only one to worry about and tend to. This marinated flank steak is tender, juicy, and, when served with a side of horseradish cream, out-of-control tasty.

Lay out the steak and sprinkle each side evenly with the salt.

In a large resealable plastic bag, combine the lager, oil, the ¼ cup horseradish, balsamic, Dijon, onion, garlic, peppercorns, parsley, thyme, and rosemary. Mash it all around to combine and then add in the steak. Press out as much air from the bag as possible before sealing and do your best to distribute the aromatics around the meat. Place the bag in the fridge on top of a baking sheet to catch any potential leaks and allow the steak to marinate for at least 5 hours, and up to 24 hours, turning the bag occasionally.

Remove the steak from the fridge 30 minutes before you want to cook it. Meanwhile, preheat your grill to medium-high. Remove your steak from the marinade, dry it off with some paper towel, and brush a little oil over it. Season with a little more salt, and grill for 7 to 8 minutes per side, or until cooked to your liking.

Transfer the steak to a cutting board, tent it with aluminum foil, and allow it to rest for about 10 minutes.

Meanwhile, prepare the horseradish cream by combining the remaining horseradish with the sour cream and Montreal steak spice in a small bowl.

Thinly slice the flank against the grain and serve with the horseradish cream.

Note:
If you can't find a flank big enough, a couple of smaller flanks will work well and still be much easier to prepare and serve than individual cuts.

Apple Butter Roast Pork

SERVES 8

1 (about 4 lb) pork loin roast, bone in or out
1 teaspoon kosher salt, divided
1 teaspoon freshly ground black pepper, divided
½ cup unsweetened apple butter
3 tablespoons smooth Dijon mustard
1 teaspoon apple cider vinegar
¼ teaspoon ground cinnamon

This is one of those magical recipes that you can whip up either on a regular old Tuesday just for you and the fam or when you're looking to pull out the big guns. I always feel like this would be my go-to if my boss were coming round to dinner. It's so simple and, depending on whether you get a pork loin with bone in or not, it can be as pretty as a picture or as regal as the queen's handbag.

Preheat your oven to 350°F and place the pork loin roast, fat side up, in a roasting pan lined with a wire rack. Season the whole outside of the pork with ½ teaspoon each of the salt and pepper and set aside.

In a small bowl, mix together the remaining salt and pepper, the apple butter, Dijon, vinegar, and cinnamon. Using a pastry brush or the back of a spoon, coat the entire outside of the pork with this apple butter mixture (you'll need to keep some for basting) and pour just enough water into the pan to cover the bottom without allowing it to touch the pork loin.

Roast the pork until its internal temperature reaches 145°F, about 1 hour and 15 minutes, basting with some more of the apple butter after the first 30 minutes. If you notice that the water below the pork is running dry, add a splash more every once in a while. If the roast is browning too quickly, cover it loosely with aluminum foil while it continues to cook.

Transfer the pork to a cutting board to rest for about 10 minutes before serving and slicing at the table.

Note:
To get ahead, glaze the pork up to 1 day before cooking it.

Pancetta Pork Tenderloin

SERVES 8–10

FOR THE MARINADE

1 cup hard cider
⅓ cup smooth Dijon mustard
⅓ cup pure maple syrup
¼ cup olive oil
1 tablespoon kosher salt
1 teaspoon coarsely ground black pepper
8 sprigs thyme
4 sprigs rosemary
4 cloves garlic
3 (each 1 lb) pork tenderloins
1 small cooking onion, thinly sliced

FOR THE ROAST

2 cloves garlic, minced
2 tablespoons finely chopped fresh rosemary leaves
2 tablespoons finely chopped fresh thyme leaves
1½ teaspoons kosher salt
½ teaspoon freshly ground black pepper
2 tablespoons olive oil
36 thin slices pancetta (about 7 oz in total)

Note:
The pork can be marinated 2 days ahead and wrapped in the pancetta the night before or morning of. The tenderloins will hold if properly covered in the fridge, but be sure to bring them out of the fridge about 20 or 30 minutes before roasting them.

I feel like pork tenderloin is the new chicken in terms of being a cheap, easy, and tender staple at the dinner table. There are countless ways to prepare it, but marinating it overnight and then wrapping in herbs and pancetta gives this lean cut of meat the oomph it needs to really make it a fan favorite.

For the marinade, combine the cider, Dijon, maple syrup, oil, salt, and pepper in a large bowl or a large heavy-duty resealable plastic bag and mash it around to bring it all together. Using the back of a large knife, whack the thyme and rosemary a few times to bruise it all up a bit. This will help the herbs release more of their flavor in the marinade. Smash and roughly chop the garlic and add it, along with the herbs, tenderloins, and onions, to the marinade. Make sure the pork is completely submerged and cover or seal it all up to sit in the fridge for at least 2 hours, or up to 24 hours, to allow the flavors to marry.

When you're ready to cook, remove the pork from the marinade, dry it off with some paper towel, and allow it to sit at room temperature for 20 to 30 minutes.

Preheat your oven to 425°F, line a baking sheet or roasting pan with a wire rack, and get to work on your pancetta wrap.

For the roast, in a small bowl, mix together the garlic, rosemary, thyme, salt, pepper, and oil. Set aside.

Arrange 12 pancetta slices on a work surface so that they overlap slightly and form a rectangle. Evenly scatter one-third of the herb and garlic mixture over the pancetta (see fig.1) and place 1 pork tenderloin along the center. Wrap the two sides around the pork tenderloin (fig.2), flip it over, and place on the rack-lined pan. Repeat this step with the other 2 tenderloins, making sure to leave some space between each on the pan.

Roast the pork tenderloins for 30 to 35 minutes, or until the internal temperature reaches 145°F.

Allow the pork to rest for 10 minutes under a loose piece of aluminum foil before slicing it into 1-inch pieces for serving.

TOP LEFT OF IMAGE: TOMATO OVEN RISOTTO (PAGE 137)

1

2

TOP LEFT OF IMAGE: PECORINO PANKO-ROASTED MUSHROOMS (PAGE 141)

Maple Miso Spatchcocked Chickens

SERVES 8–10

2 (each 3½–4 lb) chickens, patted dry
¼ cup unsalted butter
⅓ cup red miso paste
⅓ cup pure maple syrup
3 cloves garlic, minced
1 teaspoon kosher salt
½ teaspoon freshly ground black pepper
1 tablespoon vegetable oil

Spatchcock: a fancy word for flattened poultry. By removing the backbone of the bird and squashing it down flat, roast chicken is suddenly possible in under 1 hour. If that isn't enough to impress, the maple-miso glaze adds the perfect hit of smoky umami.

Preheat your oven to 425°F and spatchcock your chickens by removing their backbones with a pair of kitchen shears. Flip the birds over so that they're breast side up and press down on the breastbone until you feel a pop. You've just flattened the chickens.

In a small bowl, combine the butter, miso paste, maple syrup, garlic, salt, and pepper. Flip the chickens over so that they're breast side down and line a baking sheet or roasting pan with a wire rack. Brush the inside of the chickens with about one-third of the maple-miso mixture and place them, breast side up, on the rack. Drizzle the chicken skin with the oil and roast for 20 minutes. Open the oven door and carefully brush the remaining maple-miso mixture all over the skin and then roast for another 20 to 30 minutes, or until the juices run clear and the thickest part of the thighs register 165°F on a meat thermometer. Remove the chickens from the oven, loosely tent them with aluminum foil, and allow them to rest for about 10 minutes prior to serving.

Note:
If you're nervous about spatchcocking your own chickens, your butcher should be able to do it for you.

Slow-Roasted Salmon with Tarragon-Chive Mayonnaise

SERVES 8

1 (3 lb) salmon fillet
4 tablespoons extra virgin olive oil, divided
2 tablespoons smooth Dijon mustard
2 teaspoons kosher salt
½–1 teaspoon dried chili flakes
1 lemon, zested and halved
½ cup mayonnaise
¼ cup finely chopped fresh tarragon leaves
¼ cup finely chopped fresh chives
Kosher salt
Freshly ground black pepper
Lemon wedges, for serving

When making fish for a crowd, I always go with a whole fillet rather than portions. It is by far the most foolproof method and looks pretty darn majestic sitting on the table surrounded by a big dish of tarragon-chive mayo and all the fixings. Slow-roasting the fish gives you a fillet that could never in a million years be described as dry. Just don't expect the skin to be crispy.

Preheat your oven to 300°F and dry off the salmon fillet by dabbing it with paper towel. Coat the bottom of a baking sheet with 2 tablespoons of the oil and place the salmon, skin side down, on the sheet. Rub the flesh side of the salmon with the remaining oil and brush the Dijon evenly over top. Sprinkle with the salt and chili flakes and squeeze one lemon half over top.

Bake the salmon until it's slightly firm and springy to the touch or the center just flakes when tested with a fork, 28 to 35 minutes, depending on the fillet's thickness.

Meanwhile, squeeze the juice from the remaining lemon half into a small bowl. Add in the zest, mayonnaise, tarragon, and chives. Mix to combine. Season with salt and pepper and set aside.

Remove the salmon from the oven and place it on a platter with the tarragon-chive mayonnaise. Garnish with lemon wedges. To serve, use a spatula or fish server to cut portions, leaving the skin behind.

Note:
This dish is so, so good served cold; it's the perfect make-ahead dinner.

Red Wine-Braised English-Cut Short Ribs

SERVES 8

- 8 (each 4–5 inches long) English-cut short ribs
- 2 tablespoons finely chopped fresh rosemary
- 2 tablespoons finely chopped fresh thyme
- 2 teaspoons kosher salt
- 1 teaspoon freshly cracked black pepper
- 2 tablespoons vegetable oil
- 2 small cooking onions, halved and quartered
- 4 cloves garlic, smashed
- 1 carrot, cut into large chunks
- 2 bay leaves
- 1 bottle dry red wine, such as cabernet sauvignon
- 2 cups no- or low-sodium beef broth
- 3 tablespoons unsalted butter
- 3 tablespoons all-purpose flour

Drunk with red wine and herbs, the only thing difficult about these English-cut short ribs is trying to plate them with the bone still attached. Seriously, the term "fall off the bone" doesn't even begin to describe how wonderfully tender these guys are.

The night before you plan on cooking the short ribs, season them with the rosemary, thyme, salt, and pepper. Place them in a baking pan, cover with aluminum foil, and refrigerate overnight, or for up to 24 hours.

Take the short ribs out of the fridge and leave them at room temperature for about 1 hour while you preheat your oven to 375°F and prep the rest of your ingredients.

Once the ribs have warmed up, place a Dutch oven over medium-high heat. Heat the oil and sear the ribs for about 2 minutes per side to develop a good crust. Place them back in the pan they were stored in and then place the onions, garlic, carrots, and bay leaves in the Dutch oven. Give everything a stir, turn down the heat to medium, and cook for about 1 minute. Deglaze the pot with the wine and add in the broth. Add the ribs back to the pot, along with any juices and herbs that may have collected in the pan, and bring the mixture to a simmer. Cover the Dutch oven with its lid and place in the oven to cook undisturbed for 2 hours.

Carefully remove the ribs from their braising liquid, place them in a deep plate or baking pan, and cover with aluminum foil to keep warm. Strain out and discard (or snack on!) the vegetables and pour the liquid back into the Dutch oven.

In a small pot, melt the butter over medium heat. Sprinkle the flour over the butter and whisk constantly to form a roux. Cook the roux for about 1 to 2 minutes, or until it has a little color. Whisk about 1 cup of the braising liquid into the roux and then add the mixture to the Dutch oven. Whisk to combine and bring everything to a boil. Reduce the liquid until it is thick enough to coat the back of a spoon.

Reheat the ribs in the thickened braising liquid. Serve the ribs and sauce over anything your heart desires. You wouldn't be wrong to pair them with Blue Cheese Polenta (page 132), Secret Ingredient Mashed Potatoes (page 187), or Mashed Butternut Squash with Crispy Sage (page 199).

Note:

This recipe can be mostly prepared ahead. After straining the braising liquid, place it back in the Dutch oven along with the ribs. Allow it to cool to room temperature and then cover and refrigerate for 1 to 2 days. To reheat, remove the hard layer of fat that may have formed on top of the braising liquid, cover, and bring the ribs and liquid to a simmer over medium-low heat for about 20 to 30 minutes. Transfer the ribs to a plate to keep warm while you make the roux and thicken the sauce according to the method. Finish and serve as directed.

Root Vegetable Tarte Tatin

SERVES 8

- 3–4 carrots
- 3–4 large parsnips
- 1 butternut squash
- 2 small red onions
- 2 red beets
- 3 tablespoons olive oil
- 1 teaspoon kosher salt
- ½ teaspoon freshly ground black pepper
- ½ cup granulated sugar
- 1½ tablespoons apple cider vinegar
- 2 teaspoons finely chopped fresh thyme leaves
- 2 teaspoons finely chopped fresh sage leaves
- 4½ oz soft goat cheese
- 1 sheet frozen puff pastry, thawed

Note:
To avoid bright pink hands, wear a pair of disposable gloves while peeling and slicing the beets. If you don't have any, I find that a little lemon juice, some salt, and good old-fashioned elbow grease works wonders to remove stains.

Few things strike fear into a host like dietary restrictions. I myself am a pescatarian and have seen the panic in a host's eyes as they try to think of a main dish to serve to the non-meat eaters in the crowd. Well, this tarte tatin is here to save the day. It's a perfect main dish for vegetarians that all of the meat eaters will be reaching for.

Preheat your oven to 400°F and peel and cut the carrots, parsnips, and squash into 1-inch slices. Peel and cut the onions and beets into ½-inch slices. Spread the vegetables onto one or two baking sheets and drizzle with the oil. Season with the salt and pepper and roast for 25 to 35 minutes, giving them a flip about halfway through. Remove the veg from the oven and allow them to cool slightly while you prepare the savory caramel. Leave the oven on.

For the caramel, pour the sugar into a small pot and add in 3 tablespoons of water. Without stirring, place this over medium heat and cook, still not stirring, until the sugar dissolves and turns a lovely golden color, about 5 to 7 minutes. Keep a close eye on it so the sugar doesn't burn.

Meanwhile, grease a 9- × 13-inch baking pan with nonstick cooking spray and set aside.

When the caramel is a deep golden color, quickly remove it from the heat and carefully pour in the vinegar. Swirl the pot around to combine, then drizzle into the prepared baking pan. The caramel probably won't cover the whole pan, but just drizzle it in so that it's evenly distributed. Scatter or place the roasted vegetables on top of the caramel in an even layer, sprinkle with the thyme and sage, dot with the goat cheese, and set aside.

On a lightly floured work surface, roll the pastry into a rectangle that is about 9 × 13 inches. Drape the pastry over the vegetables and bake for 20 minutes. Turn down the heat to 350°F and continue cooking for 15 to 20 minutes, or until the pastry is golden brown.

Allow the tatin to cool for 3 minutes before carefully inverting it onto a wooden cutting board or serving dish.

Blue Cheese Polenta

SERVES 6–8

- 8 cups no- or low-sodium chicken or vegetable broth
- 3 cloves garlic, finely minced
- 2 teaspoons kosher salt
- 2 cups yellow cornmeal
- ¼ cup unsalted butter
- 1 cup finely grated Parmigiano-Reggiano cheese
- 4½–5 oz crumbled blue cheese, such as Roquefort or Gorgonzola Piccante
- ½ cup finely chopped flat-leaf parsley
- Kosher salt
- Freshly ground black pepper

I've never understood the toilsome stories of polenta making. I feel like there is an inherent fear that surrounds a dish when you hear nonnas spinning reverential tales of sweating over the stove for hours, stirring and stirring a bubbling pot of what is essentially cornmeal and broth. Maybe I've been making it wrong my whole life, but a pot of polenta has never taken me more than 20 minutes to whip up. It's about as easy as stovetop mac and cheese and approximately 8,000 times more delicious.

In a large pot with a tight-fitting lid, bring the broth to a boil over high heat. Add in the garlic and salt and get the lid ready.

While whisking vigorously, slowly pour in the cornmeal, quickly pop the lid on, and turn down the heat to low. Be careful here, as the polenta does like to bubble quite a bit. If it starts bubbling over, keep the pot covered and take it off the heat for a few seconds.

Cook the polenta for about 20 minutes, giving it a good stir every 5 to 7 minutes or so to make sure it's not sticking to the bottom of the pan. Once it's thick and creamy, add the butter, followed by both cheeses and the parsley, and stir well to combine. Check for seasoning and add salt and pepper to taste.

Serve immediately, or keep warm in the covered pot over low heat. If the polenta thickens up too much while it sits, just add a splash of water, broth, or cream and whisk vigorously to combine.

Note:
If you'd like to make this ahead, prepare the polenta as above and then pour it into a greased 9- x 13-inch pan to set up in the fridge. Slice the polenta into servings and fry it all up in some butter or oil to serve.

Squashed Potatoes with Gremolata and Feta

SERVES 8–10

- 2½–3 lb baby potatoes
- ¼ cup + 2 tablespoons olive oil, divided
- 1½ teaspoons kosher salt, plus more for the potato water
- 1 teaspoon freshly ground black pepper
- 2 cloves garlic, minced
- ¼ cup finely chopped flat-leaf parsley
- 3 tablespoons finely chopped chives
- Grated zest and juice of 1 lemon
- 7 oz feta cheese, crumbled

There is this incredible little café a few doors down from Snug Harbor on Frenchmen Street in New Orleans called Three Muses. I was first drawn in by the sounds of a muted trumpet, but what kept me coming back during my trip were the most amazing french fries I'd ever eaten: perfectly golden and crisp, and topped with herby gremolata and mounds of crumbly feta. Here, if you swap the fries for crispy roasted potatoes, you've got some jazzy spuds for your dinner table.

Preheat your oven to 425°F.

Place the baby potatoes in a large pot of cold salted water and bring to a boil over high heat. Cook until fork-tender, about 10 to 12 minutes, strain, and allow the potatoes to cool slightly. When they're cool enough to handle, use the heel of your hand to squash each potato down slightly just so it bursts and flattens a bit. Transfer the potatoes to a large baking sheet, drizzle with the ¼ cup of oil and season with salt and pepper. Roast for 15 to 20 minutes, flip, and cook for another 10 to 15 minutes, or until the potatoes are golden and crispy.

Meanwhile, to make the gremolata, combine the remaining oil, the garlic, parsley, chives, and lemon zest and juice in a small bowl and set aside.

When the potatoes are done, transfer them to a serving bowl and top with the herby gremolata and a good scattering of feta.

Note:
To get ahead, boil and roast your potatoes the day before you plan to serve them. To serve, refry the potatoes in a frying pan with a glug of olive oil and top with the gremolata and feta.

Tomato Oven Risotto

SERVES 8–10

- 2 small cooking onions, diced
- 2 tablespoons olive oil
- 3 cloves garlic, minced
- 3 cups Arborio rice
- 1 cup dry white wine
- 1 (28 oz) can crushed tomatoes
- 2 teaspoons kosher salt
- 2 teaspoons freshly ground black pepper
- 4½ cups no- or low-sodium chicken or vegetable broth, divided
- 2 cups cherry tomatoes, halved
- 2 tablespoons balsamic vinegar
- 1 cup sundried tomatoes in oil, chopped
- ½ cup chopped flat-leaf parsley
- ¼ cup chopped fresh basil
- 2 cups grated Parmigiano-Reggiano cheese, plus some shaved for garnish

SEE IMAGE ON PAGE 123

I am here to banish the myth that risotto is a tricky, time-consuming dish to make. Yes, traditional stovetop risotto does take a good amount of stirring, but this here is oven risotto. It is truly a simple one-pot dish that requires nothing more than some chopping, sautéing, one or two stirs, and a trip to the oven.

Preheat your oven to 350°F.

In a Dutch oven set over medium heat, cook the onions in the oil until translucent, about 2 to 3 minutes. Add in the garlic and cook for another minute. Add in the rice and cook, stirring frequently, for about 1 to 2 minutes to toast it. Pour in the wine and stir until it has been absorbed. Stir in the crushed tomatoes, salt, and pepper, followed by 3½ cups of the broth, the cherry tomatoes, and balsamic. Bring the risotto to a simmer, cover with the lid, and bake in the oven for 45 minutes.

Remove the risotto from the oven and give it a vigorous stir. If needed, add the remaining broth, ¼ cup at a time, to loosen the risotto and make it nice and creamy. Stir in the sundried tomatoes, parsley, and basil, followed by the cheese. Serve topped with some shaved Parm.

Roasted Napa Cabbage

SERVES 8

FOR THE CABBAGE

1 Napa cabbage, cut into 8 wedges
3 tablespoons extra virgin olive oil
1 teaspoon ground cumin
½ teaspoon cayenne pepper
½ teaspoon kosher salt
¼ teaspoon freshly ground black pepper

FOR THE DRESSING

¼ cup olive oil
3 tablespoons lemon juice
1 tablespoon red wine vinegar
1 teaspoon ground cumin
½ teaspoon dried chili flakes
½ teaspoon smoked paprika
½ teaspoon grated lemon zest
Kosher salt
Finely ground black pepper

I'd like to take this moment to thank whoever brought kale chips into the limelight. Sure, they're healthier than potato chips while still delivering that salty crunch we crave, but to me, the whole idea of flash-roasting leafy cabbage is stinking brilliant! A little bit of oil and the high oven temperature cut the bitter notes of cabbage back and help highlight the earthy notes of this humble little plant. But I think it's about time that some other members of the Brassica *oleracea* family got their time in the oven. When you roast big wedges of Napa cabbage, the crunchy center ribs become sweet and tender and the outer leaves get shrivelly and crisp. If the weather permits, try grilling the Napa—you'll end up with the smokiest, most delicious cabbage you've ever tasted.

Preheat your oven to 450°F and place the cabbage wedges on a baking sheet. Drizzle each side of the wedges with the oil and season with the cumin, cayenne, salt, and pepper. Roast the cabbage for 10 to 15 minutes, or until the edges are golden brown, flipping halfway through.

Meanwhile, prepare the dressing by whisking together the oil, lemon juice, vinegar, cumin, chili flakes, paprika, and zest. Give it a taste and season with salt and pepper.

Drizzle the warm cabbage with the dressing and serve warm or at room temperature.

Pecorino Panko-Roasted Mushrooms

SERVES 8

- 8 cups oyster mushrooms
- 3 cloves garlic, finely minced
- 5 tablespoons olive oil, divided
- 2 tablespoons balsamic vinegar
- Kosher salt
- Freshly ground black pepper
- ½ cup finely grated Pecorino cheese
- ¼ cup panko crumbs

SEE IMAGE ON PAGE 124

I *love* mushrooms. From spring to fall, you can often find me crouched down, slinking my way through wooded areas just north of the city, looking for any fascinating fungi I can find. In terms of their culinary uses, I can't think of a wrong way to cook mushrooms, but roasting has got to be one of the best.

Preheat your oven to 425°F, gently wipe any dirt from the mushrooms with a damp cloth, and scatter the mushrooms onto a large baking sheet.

In a small bowl, whisk together the garlic, 2 tablespoons of the oil, and the balsamic, and toss with the mushrooms. Season with salt and pepper and set aside.

In a small bowl, mix together the remaining oil, the cheese, and panko, and season with salt and pepper. Scatter this crunchy topping evenly over top the mushrooms and bake for 5 to 10 minutes, or until golden and a little crispy.

Raspberry Shortcakes with White Chocolate Lemon Curd

SERVES 8

FOR THE CURD

4 eggs
¾ cup granulated sugar
¾ cup lemon juice (about 4 lemons)
1 tablespoon grated lemon zest
¼ teaspoon fine salt
¼ cup unsalted butter
¾ cup white chocolate chips

FOR THE SHORTCAKES

2 cups all-purpose flour
3 tablespoons granulated sugar
1½ tablespoons baking powder
¼ teaspoon baking soda
¾ teaspoon kosher salt
½ cup unsalted butter, straight from the fridge
1 cup buttermilk, straight from the fridge
½ teaspoon pure vanilla extract
1 cup fresh raspberries
2 tablespoons melted butter
Turbinado sugar (optional)
Whipped cream (optional)

There are a few things that a dessert needs for me to really go bonkers over it. It should be a little tart, it can't be too sweet, and a smattering of fruit is always appreciated. That's what makes these shortcakes so perfect in my books. Sweet white chocolate tames the tartness of the lemon curd, while slightly sour raspberries bake into jammy bits throughout the shortcakes. No part of this is too sweet, tart, or overpowering, so even after a big meal, your guests will be tempted to lick their dessert plates clean.

For the curd, combine the eggs, sugar, lemon juice and zest, and salt in a small pot and cook over medium heat, stirring frequently with a whisk, until thick, about 10 minutes. Once it's thick, whisk in the butter, about 1 tablespoon at a time, and then whisk in the white chocolate chips. When the chocolate has melted in, remove the curd from the heat, pass it through a fine mesh sieve into a bowl, cover the surface directly with plastic wrap, and chill in the fridge until ready to use.

For the shortcakes, preheat your oven to 425°F and line a baking sheet with parchment paper.

In a large bowl, combine the flour, sugar, baking powder, baking soda, and salt. Remove your butter from the fridge and cut it into small pieces. Quickly combine the cold butter into the dry ingredients by rubbing the mixture between your hands until it resembles very coarse crumbs with some larger chunks of butter scattered throughout. Make a well in the center of the mixture, pour in the buttermilk and vanilla, and stir just until combined. Dump the dough out onto a well-floured work surface, scatter the raspberries on top, and dust with a little more flour. Gently press the dough down with the palms of your hands, then fold it over onto itself. Do this four or five more times.

Form the dough into a rough circle and place it on your prepared baking sheet. Cut the circle of dough into eight with a floured knife, leaving all of the pieces touching. Brush the whole round with melted butter and sprinkle with turbinado sugar (if using).

Bake your shortcakes for 18 to 22 minutes, or until golden brown and springy to the touch. Let cool slightly, separate the shortcakes, and serve with way too much of that delicious white chocolate lemon curd, maybe a few extra raspberries, and a dollop of whipped cream.

Food Processor Flourless Chocolate Cake

MAKES 1 (8-INCH) CAKE

FOR THE CAKE

- 1 tablespoon + ¼ cup cocoa powder
- 10½ oz dark chocolate, at least 55% cocoa
- 1 cup granulated sugar
- ¾ cup very hot coffee
- 6 eggs, separated
- 1 cup unsalted butter
- 1 tablespoon pure vanilla extract
- Grated zest of 1 orange
- 1 teaspoon kosher salt

FOR THE TOPPING

- 1 cup mascarpone
- 1 cup whipping (35%) cream
- ¼ cup icing sugar
- ½ teaspoon pure vanilla extract
- Grated zest of 1 orange, divided
- 2 tablespoons granulated sugar
- 1 tablespoon orange liqueur or orange juice
- 2 pints of whatever fruit your heart desires

Food processors aren't really used much in the world of cake making, but somehow this just works. The perfect chocolate cake for entertaining, this little number is best made a day or two in advance so that it has time to rest and get extra fudgy. All you need to do to serve is whip some mascarpone cream and scatter some berries, leaving you as the host with a relaxed, breezy, "oh, this little thing?" air.

Preheat your oven to 350°F, grease an 8-inch springform pan with cooking spray, and dust the inside with the 1 tablespoon of cocoa.

For the cake, place the remaining cocoa, the chocolate, and sugar in the bowl of a food processor fitted with the steel blade and blitz until finely ground and combined. Pour in the hot coffee and process until smooth. Add in the egg yolks, butter, vanilla, orange zest, and salt and blitz to combine. Transfer to a bowl and set aside.

Meanwhile, whip the egg whites to stiff peaks and fold about one-third of them into the chocolate mixture. Fold in the remaining whites, taking care to be very gentle in order to maintain as much volume as possible. Pour the mixture into your prepared pan and bake for 40 to 50 minutes, until souffléd and the top of the cake looks dry and matte. Let the cake cool to room temperature and then refrigerate overnight to settle.

When you're ready to serve, make the topping. Whip together the mascarpone, cream, icing sugar, vanilla, and half of the orange zest until light and fluffy. Set aside. In a separate bowl, combine the remaining orange zest, granulated sugar, orange liqueur (or juice) and fruit. Dollop this mascarpone cream onto the chilled cake and top with the fruit.

Note:

The top of the cake will fall once you take it out of the oven, but that's all part of the plan. It makes for a super-fudgy cake with lots of room for topping with mascarpone cream and berries. A 9-inch springform pan will also work here; just check for doneness at the 40-minute mark.

Double Chocolate Almond Biscotti

MAKES 30 BISCOTTI

- ½ cup unsalted butter
- ¾ cup granulated sugar
- 2 eggs
- 1½ teaspoons pure vanilla extract
- ½ teaspoon pure almond extract
- ¼ teaspoon instant espresso powder
- 1¾ cups + 2 tablespoons all-purpose flour
- ¼ cup + 2 tablespoons cocoa powder
- 1½ teaspoons baking powder
- ½ teaspoon fine sea salt
- ¾ cup whole almonds, blanched or raw
- 1½ cups semi-sweet chocolate chips

Note:
If you want to serve this with affogato, brew some espresso or very strong coffee. Place 2 small scoops of vanilla ice cream in a coffee cup and then pour a shot of espresso (or about ¼ cup of strong coffee) over top. Serve with biscotti for dunking and a spoon for scooping.

Biscotti get a bum rap in the world of cookies. They're dry and crumbly, and always seem to be an afterthought, ordered only when staring you in the face while you're paying for a coffee at your local café. Well, I think it's about time that biscotti got their day in the sun. Homemade is gads better than any I've ever purchased, and one batch whips up enough to share. If you want to fancy it up a bit, pull an Aaron Mariash, and serve these cookies with affogato.

In a large bowl, cream the butter with the sugar until light and fluffy, about 2 to 3 minutes. Beat in the eggs, one at a time, until fully combined. In a small bowl, mix the vanilla and almond extracts with the espresso powder and then beat the mixture into the butter.

In a separate bowl, sift together the flour, cocoa, baking powder, and salt and stir in the almonds. Add the dry ingredients to the wet and stir just until combined. Place the bowl in the fridge to chill for 30 minutes.

Meanwhile, preheat the oven to 350°F and line one large or two small baking sheets with parchment paper. Once the dough has chilled, divide it in half and form each piece into a rectangle, approximately 3 × 8 inches, on the prepared sheets. If you're using only one baking sheet, be sure to leave at least 5 inches between the two biscotti loaves, as they will rise and spread in the oven. Bake for 25 to 30 minutes, or until springy and firm—they won't change color.

Remove the biscotti loaves from the oven and allow them to cool slightly on the baking sheet for 10 to 15 minutes. Turn down the oven to 325°F and slice each loaf into about 15 cookies. I like to do mine on a bit of an angle—it gives you longer and nicer-looking biscotti. Place the biscotti cut side down on the baking sheet(s) and bake for another 15 minutes. Flip them over and bake for an additional 5 minutes.

Remove the biscotti from the oven and allow them to cool on a wire rack while you melt the chocolate in the microwave in 30-second increments. Once the biscotti are cool, dunk or drizzle each cookie with the chocolate and allow it to set up on a piece of parchment before digging in.

Berry Orange Slump

SERVES 6–8

FOR THE FRUIT

6 tablespoons granulated sugar
1 tablespoon cornstarch
½ teaspoon ground cinnamon
⅛ teaspoon grated nutmeg
1 tablespoon grated orange zest
½ cup orange juice
3 cups trimmed and quartered strawberries
1 cup fresh raspberries
1 cup fresh blackberries
1 cup fresh blueberries
1 teaspoon pure vanilla extract

FOR THE SLUMP TOPPING

½ cup all-purpose flour
½ cup whole wheat flour
3 tablespoons granulated sugar
2 teaspoons baking powder
¼ teaspoon baking soda
¼ teaspoon fine salt
⅛ teaspoon freshly grated nutmeg
½ cup + 2 tablespoons buttermilk
2 tablespoons unsalted butter, melted
2 teaspoons turbinado or raw sugar

Ice cream, for serving

Slump, cobbler, buckle, or grunt. No matter what you call this humble style of dessert, there is no denying that it is delicious. Essentially a pan of cooked fruit topped with biscuits or crumble, this folksy charmer is welcome at the end of any meal.

Preheat your oven to 400°F.

For the fruit, in a bowl or a glass measuring cup, whisk together the sugar, cornstarch, cinnamon, and nutmeg. Add the orange zest and then the orange juice and pour the mixture into a 9- or 10-inch cast iron skillet. Place the skillet over medium-high heat and bring the mixture to a boil, whisking frequently. Allow the mixture to cook for about 2 to 3 minutes, or until thick, add in all the berries and vanilla, and stir gently to combine. Remove the pan from the heat and set aside to cool slightly.

For the slump topping, whisk together both flours, the granulated sugar, baking powder, baking soda, salt, and nutmeg in a large bowl. Add the buttermilk and butter and stir until a moist dough forms. Carefully spoon the dough in 6 to 8 dollops over the berries and sprinkle the top with the turbinado (or raw) sugar.

Bake for 20 to 25 minutes, or until the biscuit topping is cooked through and golden brown. Allow the slump to cool a little before serving with a big scoop of your favorite ice cream.

Pear Frangipane Tart

SERVES 8–10

- 1 sheet frozen puff pastry, thawed
- 5 tablespoons unsalted butter
- ½ cup granulated sugar, divided
- 1 egg
- ½ teaspoon pure almond extract
- ½ teaspoon pure vanilla extract
- ¾ cup almond flour
- 5 teaspoons all-purpose flour
- ½ teaspoon kosher salt
- 1 teaspoon ground cinnamon, divided
- 4–5 firm, ripe d'Anjou pears, cored and thinly sliced
- ¼ cup sliced almonds
- ¼ cup apricot jam

This tart could be the long-lost cousin of an almond croissant. By using flaky puff pastry in place of a traditional tart crust, and filling it with nutty, fudgy, and almost cake-y frangipane, you get all of the textures and flavors of an almond croissant without all of the work. When you add pears into the mix, this tart is a huge hit any time of year, though, to me, it just screams fall.

Preheat your oven to 400°F and line a 10-inch tart pan with a removable bottom with the sheet of puff pastry. Trim away any overhang by running a rolling pin over the edges of the tart pan. Dock the bottom by piercing it with a fork about 20 times and then place the pan in the fridge to keep cool.

Meanwhile, in a large bowl, cream together the butter and ¼ cup of the sugar until light and fluffy, then mix in the egg and both extracts. Add in both flours, the salt, and ½ teaspoon of the cinnamon and mix just until combined. Grab the chilled pastry from the fridge, spread this frangipane evenly over the base of the pastry, and set aside.

Place the remaining sugar, remaining cinnamon, and the pears in the same bowl you used for the frangipane and give it all a gentle toss to combine. Arrange the pears on top of the frangipane in any way you see fit, then scatter the sliced almonds over top.

Place the tart on a baking sheet and bake for 30 minutes, or until the pears are tender and the crust is golden. While the tart is still hot, gently heat the jam with 1 tablespoon of water in a small pot or in the microwave. Gently daub the top of the tart with the jam to give it a sheen. Allow the tart to cool completely before serving.

Note:
Almond flour is simply finely ground almonds. If you can't find it in your grocery store, make your own by pulverizing almonds in a food processor until they are very finely ground.

Blueberry Upside-Down Lemon Cake

MAKES 1 (9-INCH) CAKE

- ½ cup unsalted butter
- 1 cup granulated sugar
- 2 eggs
- 1 cup plain yogurt
- 2 tablespoons grated lemon zest
- 1 tablespoon lemon juice
- 1½ teaspoons pure vanilla extract
- 1¾ cups all-purpose flour
- ¼ cup yellow cornmeal, plus more for your pan
- 1 tablespoon baking powder
- 1 teaspoon baking soda
- ½ teaspoon fine sea salt
- 2 cups fresh blueberries
- Icing sugar, for dusting (optional)

In my humble opinion, cakes without frosting are the best cakes. Not only are they *way* easier to make, but they are also more of an anytime cake than a traditional three-tiered extravaganza. This one in particular is a frosting-free showstopper. The golden hue of the sponge and purple of the blueberries look pretty darn regal and super delicious.

Preheat your oven to 350°F and prepare a 9-inch springform pan by spraying it with nonstick cooking spray and dusting the bottom and sides with cornmeal. Shake out any excess cornmeal and wrap the outside of the pan with aluminum foil to ensure that nothing leaks out. Set aside.

In a bowl, cream the butter with the sugar until light and fluffy, about 2 to 3 minutes. Add the eggs one at a time, mixing well between each addition. Stir in the yogurt, lemon zest and juice, and vanilla.

In a separate bowl, mix together the flour, cornmeal, baking powder, baking soda, and salt. Add this all at once to the wet ingredients. Stir just until combined.

Scatter the blueberries into the bottom of your prepared pan and pour the batter over top. Bake for 50 to 60 minutes, or until the center is springy and a toothpick inserted into it comes out clean.

Allow the cake to cool for 15 minutes in the pan and then release the sides and invert the cake onto a wire rack. Gently and carefully lift the base of the pan off the cake, being sure to leave the blueberries in place, and allow the cake to cool. Just before serving, give the cake a dusting of icing sugar or serve as is.

Chai Sticky Toffee Pudding

SERVES 10–12

FOR THE STICKY TOFFEE PUDDING

3 chai tea bags
1½ cups boiling water
2¼ cups finely chopped pitted dates
½ cup + 2 tablespoons milk
1½ teaspoons baking soda
2¼ cups all-purpose flour
1½ teaspoons baking powder
2½ teaspoons ground cinnamon
1 teaspoon ground ginger
1 teaspoon ground cardamom
½ teaspoon ground allspice
¼ teaspoon ground cloves
½ teaspoon fine sea salt
⅛ teaspoon freshly ground black pepper
½ cup unsalted butter
½ cup granulated sugar
½ cup brown sugar, packed
2 teaspoons pure vanilla extract
3 eggs

FOR THE TOFFEE SAUCE

2 cups brown sugar, packed
1½ cups whipping (35%) cream
2 tablespoons unsalted butter
1 teaspoon kosher salt
1 teaspoon pure vanilla extract

Vanilla ice cream, for serving

Sticky toffee pudding is one of those desserts that I rarely see on a menu. When I do see it, I can't resist. It's so darkly sweet, drowned in thick toffee sauce, and topped with a melting mound of vanilla ice cream. What could be better than that? Well, I think I might have found the answer. The spicy warmth of chai enhances the already amazing flavors of this classic English treat.

Preheat your oven to 350°F and prepare a large 9- × 13-inch baking dish by coating it with a thin layer of nonstick cooking spray.

Place two of the teabags in a teapot or a heatproof cup filled with the boiling water. Cover with a towel or tea cozy and allow it to steep until quite strong but still piping hot, about 5 to 7 minutes. When the tea has steeped, remove the tea bags and measure out 1¼ cups of tea. Add the dates to the tea, cover with plastic wrap, and allow the dates to reconstitute for 5 minutes. Stir in the milk and baking soda, cover again with plastic wrap, and allow to cool to room temperature.

Meanwhile, sift the flour and baking powder into a large bowl, along with the cinnamon, ginger, cardamom, allspice, cloves, salt, and pepper. Tear open the remaining tea bag and stir it in until well combined.

In a separate bowl, cream together the butter, both sugars, and vanilla until light and fluffy, about 2 to 3 minutes. Beat in the eggs, one at a time, until fully incorporated. Mix in one-third of the flour mixture, just until combined, followed by half of the date mixture. Repeat this process with another third of flour, the rest of the date mixture, and ending with the final third of flour.

Pour the batter into your prepared baking dish and bake for 40 to 50 minutes, or until the center is springy and a toothpick inserted in the center of the pudding comes out clean.

While the pudding bakes, make the toffee sauce by combining the sugar, cream, and butter in a medium pot and bringing it to a boil over medium heat, stirring frequently. Boil the toffee sauce for 3 to 4 minutes, and then remove from the heat and stir in the salt and vanilla. Keep the sauce warm over low heat until you're ready to serve.

To serve, pour half of the sauce over the warm pudding. Serve the remaining toffee sauce on the side, along with some vanilla ice cream if you're feeling extra indulgent.

Note:

The pudding and sauce can be made up to 2 days ahead. To store, tightly cover the pudding with plastic wrap and let it sit at room temperature. Transfer the sauce to an airtight container and store it in the fridge. To reheat, poke the pudding all over with a fork and pour half of the sauce over top. Cover the pudding with aluminum foil and heat in a 300°F oven for 25 to 30 minutes, or until warmed through. Reheat the remaining sauce in a pot over low heat or in the microwave for serving.

CHAI STICKY TOFFEE PUDDING (PAGE 154)

Slablova (aka Pavlova for a Crowd)

SERVES 10–12

- 6 egg whites
- ¼ teaspoon cream of tartar
- ½ teaspoon fine sea salt
- 1½ cups superfine sugar
- 1 tablespoon cornstarch
- 1½ teaspoons lemon juice
- 1½ teaspoons pure vanilla extract
- 3 cups whipping (35%) cream
- ½ cup icing sugar
- 1 vanilla bean, sliced and seeds scraped out and reserved (or 1 tablespoon pure vanilla extract)
- 4–5 cups fresh fruit (see note)

Every time I look at this recipe, I can't help but burst into laughter. "Slab" is a hilariously blunt word. Merging it with the light, ballerina-inspired "pavlova" just seems like an "opposites attract" situation. Brutish Slab, meet the light and lofty Pav.

Preheat your oven to 300°F and line a baking sheet with parchment paper.

In a freshly cleaned bowl of a stand mixer fitted with a freshly cleaned whip attachment, whip the egg whites, cream of tartar, and salt on full speed until foamy and white throughout, about 1 minute. There should be no liquid egg white in the bowl, just soft, foamy peaks that are almost the texture of bubbles in a bubble bath.

Meanwhile, in a small bowl, mix together the superfine sugar and cornstarch. With the mixer running, carefully and gradually sprinkle in the sugar mixture and continue to whip the meringue until glossy, stiff peaks form, about 3 to 4 minutes. Add in the lemon juice and vanilla and whip for a few more seconds to combine.

Scrape the meringue onto the parchment-lined baking sheet and spread it out into a rough 10- × 15-inch rectangle. Place the meringue in the oven and immediately drop the temperature to 250°F.

Without opening the oven door, bake for 1½ hours, then turn off the oven and allow the meringue and oven to cool completely before removing. While the oven cools, the top of the meringue might fall a bit, but that will soon be covered up with delicious cream and fruit.

To decorate, whip the cream, icing sugar, and vanilla bean seeds in a very cold metal bowl just until stiff peaks form, about 2 minutes. Dollop the cream on top of the meringue and decorate with fresh fruit.

Note:

I'm partial to stone fruit, berries, passion fruit, pomegranate, and mango on my pav, but use whatever is in season.

Special Occasion Menus

FOR INDULGENT TIMES

Dinner with the In-laws

Dinner with my in-laws typically takes place at Baba's. The smell of slowly cooking onions and roasting chicken fills the house, as does the sound of pierogi water bubbling away on the stove. These are the people who introduced me to the wonders of a homemade potato dumpling, convinced me of the deliciousness of the humble beet, and made me realize that I actually do kind of like chardonnay.

I really can't think of a time with Aaron's family that hasn't revolved around a meal, and that's what makes me feel connected to them. This menu is filled with flavors reminiscent of the countless meals we've shared together and is sure to be a hit with your in-laws too.

Mulled White Wine

SERVES 10–12

- 2 bottles dry white wine, such as a riesling
- 1½ cups pear nectar or good-quality pear juice (not pear cocktail)
- ¼ cup granulated sugar
- ¼ cup liquid honey
- 1 (2-inch) piece ginger, peeled and sliced
- 10 star anise
- 6 cinnamon sticks, plus more for garnish
- 1 vanilla bean, split
- 1 tablespoon whole cloves
- 1 whole orange, sliced, peel on
- 1 whole lemon, sliced, peel on
- ½–1 cup apple or pear brandy
- 1 firm pear, such as bosc or d'Anjou, thinly sliced

Note:
To serve this during warmer months, make it more like sangria by mixing all of the ingredients in a large pitcher and serving it over ice.

My in-laws aren't really cocktail people. The only standard drink at all family functions is wine, and my mother-in-law Gail's preference is white. While trying to come up with some sort of a white wine cocktail that complements this classic family feast, mulled wine kept creeping into my mind, along with doubts that it would work. But I'm happy to say that I was wrong. Lighter in body than traditional mulled wine, this mulled white wine is flavored with some of the usual spices, along with fruity brandy and a fresh pear garnish, both added just before serving.

Pour the wine and pear nectar (or juice) into a large pot or a slow cooker and stir in the sugar, honey, ginger, star anise, cinnamon sticks, vanilla bean, cloves, orange slices, and lemon slices.

Set your stove or slow cooker to low, cover, and allow the wine to mull for at least 30 minutes. You can keep the mulled wine on low to stay warm for up to 2 hours without its losing too much flavor or becoming too heavily spiced.

When you're ready to serve, pour 2 tablespoons of the brandy into each mug and top with the mulled wine. For garnish, throw in an extra cinnamon stick and a few slices of pear.

Heirloom Tomato Galette

SERVES 8–10

FOR THE PASTRY

2 cups all-purpose flour

1 teaspoon fine salt

½ teaspoon freshly ground black pepper

1 cup unsalted butter, straight from the fridge, cut into small cubes

1 egg, straight from the fridge

¼ cup milk, straight from the fridge

FOR THE TOPPING

1 cup ricotta cheese

1 tablespoon smooth Dijon mustard

1 tablespoon grainy Dijon mustard

2 cloves garlic, minced

2 tablespoons flat-leaf parsley, very finely chopped

1½ teaspoons herbes de Provence

¼ teaspoon kosher salt

¼ teaspoon freshly ground black pepper

½ cup grated Parmigiano-Reggiano cheese, divided

½ cup grated Gruyère cheese, divided

2–3 heirloom tomatoes, very thinly sliced

1½ teaspoons fresh thyme leaves

1 tablespoon olive oil

1 egg + 2 teaspoons milk, for egg wash

The first time I visited Aaron's hometown, I was (a) terrified because I'd only met his parents briefly before this weekend trip and (b) delightfully surprised at the amazing spread created by his mom, Gail. For dinner that first night she had whipped up this mile-high tomato pie that was so perfectly sweet and buttery. This is my take on that first home-cooked meal with my future in-laws.

For the pastry, place the flour, salt, and pepper in the bowl of a food processor fitted with the steel blade and quickly pulse in the cold butter. This should only take about five to eight pulses. In a small bowl, beat the egg and milk together and pour them over the flour mixture. Pulse just until a rough dough forms. If it is a little dry, add another splash of milk. Turn the dough out onto a piece of plastic wrap and press it into a flat disk, wrapping well. Refrigerate for at least 1 hour.

Meanwhile, set your oven rack to the lowest position and preheat your oven to 425°F. Line a baking sheet with parchment paper and set aside.

For the topping, in a bowl, mix together the ricotta, both Dijons, the garlic, parsley, herbes de Provence, salt, and pepper. Stir in ¼ cup of each cheese and set aside.

Retrieve the dough from the fridge and roll it out on a well-floured work surface into a large circle about ¼-inch thick. Place the dough on the prepared baking sheet and spread the ricotta mixture onto the center of the dough, leaving about a 3-inch border all the way around. Layer on the tomatoes so that they overlap, sprinkle with the remaining cheese and the thyme, and drizzle with the oil. Season with salt and pepper and fold the edges of the crust over to form the galette. Brush the pastry with the egg wash and bake on the bottom rack of your oven for 30 to 40 minutes, or until the crust is golden brown and the tomatoes are slightly shriveled. Serve immediately or at room temperature.

Potato Pierogies à la Baba

SERVES 6–8

- 6–8 yellow potatoes, peeled and quartered
- ¼ cup potato cooking water, cooled
- 1 egg
- 3 tablespoons vegetable oil
- 2–3 cups all-purpose flour
- 1 teaspoon kosher salt
- ½ cup finely diced cooking onion
- 3 tablespoons unsalted butter, divided
- ½ cup 2% cottage cheese
- ½ cup grated cheddar cheese
- 1 teaspoon kosher salt
- ½ teaspoon freshly ground black pepper

Watching Baba whip up pierogies should probably rank as one of the Seven Wonders of the World. At 102, she still makes them in droves, with flavors ranging from savory sauerkraut to sweet saskatoon berry. The classic, though, has always been my favorite. Like any good recipe from a grandparent, this one took a while to get out of her. The ingredients and method are awash with measurements like "enough potato water" and "do this until it looks right." This is my attempt at a Mariash family favorite. If the in-laws find them even half as good as the original, I will be happy!

Cook the potatoes in boiling salted water until fork-tender, about 20 to 25 minutes. Before draining them, scoop out ¼ cup of the potato cooking water and set it aside to cool. Drain the potatoes and mash them well (or pass them through a ricer), and then set aside to cool.

Scoop 1 cup of cooled mashed potatoes into a bowl and beat in the cooled potato water, egg, and oil. Add in 2 cups of the flour and the salt and knead together, adding more flour, about ¼ cup at a time, if necessary, to make a soft dough. Turn the dough out onto a well-floured work surface and knead for about 3 to 4 minutes, or until it is springy and elastic. Set the dough aside to rest at room temperature while you make the filling.

In a medium frying pan set over medium-low heat, sweat the onion in 1 tablespoon of the butter until fragrant and slightly translucent, about 3 minutes. Transfer to a large bowl along with 2 cups of the cooled mashed potatoes, the remaining butter, both cheeses, the salt, and pepper. Mix just until combined.

To shape the pierogies, I like to follow Baba's lead. Rather than rolling out the dough and cutting out circles, simply roll your dough into smaller-than-golf-ball-sized balls and flatten each one into a rough circle. Spoon about 2 teaspoons' worth of the filling into the center of each circle and fold the dough up and around the filling. Pinch the seam to close, then set aside on a well-floured baking sheet.

Bring a large pot of salted water to a boil and lightly oil a baking sheet. Cook the pierogies in batches in the boiling water until they float to the top, about 2 to 3 minutes. Transfer the pierogies to the prepared baking sheet and gently toss them about a bit to coat evenly. Serve them warm from the pot coated in a bit of melted butter, or pan-fry them for a crunchy exterior. Either way, serve these with a good helping of sour cream and Creamy Dill Mushrooms and Spinach (page 172).

Beet Terrine

SERVES 8

6–8 large red beets
Kosher salt
Freshly ground black pepper
1 cup roughly chopped basil leaves, lightly packed, divided
10½ oz soft goat cheese, divided
4 tablespoons finely chopped unsalted roasted pistachios, divided
2 tablespoons extra virgin olive oil
2 tablespoons balsamic reduction (page 81)

We didn't really do beets in our family when I was growing up. I think it was due to my mom's neat-freak tendencies and the fact that beets can be seen as a messy ingredient. It wasn't until I met Aaron that I started to appreciate this little ruby root that is ever-present in the cuisine of his Polish heritage. Roasted beets continue to be my favorite, and when they're layered with cheese in a French-ish terrine, oooooh baby, are they ever tasty.

Preheat your oven to 400°F. Trim the ends of the beets and give them a good scrub. Wrap each beet in a piece of aluminum foil and roast for 45 to 55 minutes, or until a sharp knife slides easily into the center of each beet. When they're cool enough to handle, peel them, slice them into very thin disks, and set aside.

To form your terrine, line a 9- × 5-inch loaf pan with enough plastic wrap to cover the bottom and sides, with some hanging over the edge by a few inches. Make a layer of sliced roasted beets, being sure to cover every inch of the base, and season with salt and pepper. Scatter ¼ cup of the basil over top, dot with one-quarter of the goat cheese, and sprinkle with about 1 tablespoon of the pistachios. Repeat these layers three times and finish with a final layer of beets. Bring the plastic wrap up and over the top of the terrine and wrap well.

Place two heavy cans or jars on top of the terrine to weigh it down, and refrigerate for at least 2 hours, or up to 2 days. To serve, unwrap the terrine, place a serving dish on top of the loaf pan and turn it upside down. Peel off the plastic wrap, season with a bit more salt and pepper, and give it a good drizzle of oil and balsamic reduction. If you like, top with some extra basil leaves and chopped pistachios.

Note:

You can roast your beets well in advance—they'll keep whole or sliced in the fridge for up to 1 week.

Classic Roast Chicken

SERVES 4–6

1 (4–4½ lb) chicken
½ lemon, quartered
1 head garlic, halved crosswise
2 cooking onions, peeled and quartered
10 sprigs thyme, divided
3 sprigs rosemary, divided
1 sprig sage
1 handful flat-leaf parsley, divided
3 carrots, peeled and cut into large chunks
3 ribs celery, cut into large chunks
2 tablespoons unsalted butter
1 clove garlic, minced
½ teaspoon finely chopped fresh thyme leaves
½ teaspoon finely chopped fresh rosemary leaves
½ teaspoon finely chopped fresh sage leaves
Kosher salt
Freshly ground black pepper

Note:
If you're looking to serve more people, you can double the recipe and cook both birds in the same pan, leaving a bit of room between them. The cooking times should be around the same, but always use a kitchen thermometer to check the internal temperature to be safe.

No matter what we do for dinner at Baba's house, even if we insist on bringing everything or ordering take-out, dollars to doughnuts she'll have whipped up a roast chicken just in case there isn't enough food. Her recipe never wavers, but this is my spin on the classic. It's easy enough for a Tuesday-night family dinner and delicious enough to serve for a more special occasion. After all, there really is nothing better than a roast chicken.

Preheat your oven to 425°F and pat the chicken dry with paper towel.

Stuff the cavity of the bird with the lemon quarters, ½ garlic head, and a few bits of onion, as well as 3 sprigs of the thyme, 1 sprig of the rosemary, the sage, and half of the parsley. Tie the legs together with butcher's twine and tuck the wing tips under the body of the bird.

Place the remaining garlic, onions, thyme, rosemary, and parsley in the bottom of a roasting pan along with the carrots and celery to create a roasting rack for the chicken. Nestle the bird on top and set aside while you prepare the butter.

In a small bowl, combine the butter, garlic, and chopped thyme, rosemary, sage. Season with a pinch of salt and pepper. Using a spoon, gently separate the skin of the chicken from the meat, starting at the cavity end. Take half of the butter, divide it between the breasts and mash it under the skin. Rub the remaining butter all over the outside of the bird, give your hands a good wash, and season the chicken with more salt and pepper.

Pour enough water into the pan to come one-quarter of the way up the veggies and bake the chicken, uncovered, for 1½ hours, or until the juices run clear and the internal temperature reaches 165°F.

Remove the chicken from the oven, transfer it to a cutting board or serving platter, and cover loosely with aluminum foil. Let it rest for 15 to 20 minutes before serving.

Creamy Dill Mushrooms and Spinach

SERVES 8

- 3 tablespoons unsalted butter
- 4 cups button or cremini mushrooms, cleaned and sliced or quartered
- 2 cloves garlic, minced
- 1–2 tablespoons lemon juice
- ½ cup half and half (12%) cream
- ¼ cup sour cream
- 3 handfuls baby spinach, roughly chopped
- 2 tablespoons chopped fresh dill
- Kosher salt
- Freshly ground black pepper

If there's one thing the Mariashes have taught me, it's how to top a pierogi. Prior to family dinners with my in-laws, I always thought that my only option was a dollop of sour cream and maybe a scattering of crispy bacon and green onions. While they'd never turn their noses up at those selections, it isn't a Mariash dinner without at least three different saucy options for your pierogies. My favorite is this dilly mushroom sauce that Baba always whips up in a flash. This works well as a general side dish too.

Melt the butter in a large frying pan over medium-high heat and cook the mushrooms until golden, about 4 to 5 minutes. Turn down the heat to medium-low, add in the garlic and lemon juice, and cook for 1 to 2 minutes. Stir in the half and half, sour cream, spinach, and dill. Season to taste with salt and pepper and cook just until the spinach is wilted, about 1 minute. Serve as an accompaniment to Potato Pierogies à la Baba (page 166).

Apple Raspberry Ginger Pie

MAKES 1 (9-INCH) PIE

FOR THE PASTRY

2 cups all-purpose flour
1 tablespoon granulated sugar
1 teaspoon fine sea salt
1 cup cold unsalted butter, cut into small pieces
1 egg
3–4 tablespoons cold milk

FOR THE FILLING

2 tablespoons unsalted butter
7–8 apples, a mix of Macintosh and Granny Smith, peeled, cored, and chopped
1 tablespoon lemon juice
½ cup granulated sugar
½ cup brown sugar, packed
1 teaspoon ground cinnamon
½ teaspoon ground ginger
¼ teaspoon freshly grated nutmeg
⅛ teaspoon fine sea salt
2 tablespoons all-purpose flour
1 tablespoon cornstarch
2 tablespoons rolled oats
1 cup raspberries, fresh or frozen (thawed and drained)
1 egg + 2 teaspoons milk, for egg wash
Turbinado sugar (optional)

In my husband's family, Baba's apple pie is legendary, rivaled only by her rhubarb cake, if you ask me. Now, I am not one to rock the boat or mess with a 102-year-old Polish lady, but my apple raspberry pie is pretty darn tasty. It's crisp, sweet, and just tart enough, and it reminds me of a big comfy sweater which, now that I think of it, is what Baba hugs feel like.

For the pastry, in the bowl of a food processor fitted with the steel blade, pulse the flour, sugar, and salt. Add in the butter pieces and pulse them into the flour about five to eight times, or until they are broken up into hazelnut-sized pieces. In a small bowl, whisk together the egg and 3 tablespoons of the milk and add it to the flour mixture. Pulse the dough another three or four times to incorporate. The dough should look like a bit of a mess at this point, but if you pick some up in your hand and squeeze, it should hold together. Add the remaining milk if it's too dry.

Place a piece of plastic wrap on your work surface and dump the dough on top. Wrap everything up and press it into a 1-inch-thick round. Refrigerate the dough for 30 to 45 minutes to allow the flour to hydrate and to re-chill the fat.

Meanwhile, make the filling. Melt the butter in a large frying pan or pot over medium-high heat. Add the apples and lemon juice, followed by both sugars, the cinnamon, ginger, nutmeg, and salt, and stir to combine. Cook the apples for 5 to 7 minutes, stirring occasionally, just to soften them and allow them to start releasing their juices. Sprinkle the flour and cornstarch over the apples and stir in. Cook for 2 to 5 minutes so that the flour and cornstarch start to suck up the apple juices.

Remove the apples from the heat and allow them to cool to room temperature. When the apples are cool, preheat your oven to 425°F.

Divide your pie dough in half. Roll one half out into a ¼-inch-thick circle and place it in a 9-inch pie plate. Scatter the oats evenly across the bottom of the pastry and top with half of the apple mixture. Scatter

CONTINUES

half of the raspberries over top, followed by the remaining apples and then the remaining raspberries. Roll out the second half of dough so that it sits comfortably atop the base, cut a small steam vent into the center, and drape it over the top of the pie. Crimp the edges of the top and bottom crusts together to seal them and brush the top of the pie with the egg wash. Scatter a little turbinado sugar over top (if using).

Place the pie on a baking sheet and bake for 20 minutes. Turn down the oven to 350°F and bake for another 40 to 45 minutes, or until golden brown.

Allow the pie to cool and serve warm or at room temperature.

Note:
To make a lattice top for your pie, roll out the second half of dough and cut it into strips. Lay out half of the strips vertically across the top of your pie, then weave in the remaining strips horizontally. Trim and crimp the edges to seal, brush the pie with egg wash, and bake as instructed.

Holidays with the Family

I *love* the holidays. Every single part of the season makes me feel just as giddy and excited as I did when I was a kid! Outside of my weird obsession with wrapping gifts and my preference for cold weather and snow, the holidays are a time for all of the food and all of the family. While the classic Christmas feast will always hold a special place in my heart, this is my revamped, simplified version. It still has all of those flavors you crave, without the worry of "Did I remember to take the turkey out of the freezer?"

Cranberry Ginger Rosemary Bellini

SERVES 10

- ½ cup granulated sugar
- 2 sprigs rosemary, plus more for garnish
- 1 (3-inch) piece ginger, peeled and cut into thin disks
- 2 cups pure cranberry juice (not cocktail), chilled
- 1 bottle prosecco, chilled
- Frozen cranberries, for garnish

SEE IMAGE ON PAGE 193

White wine and red wine are great, but we here in the Berg/Foote family are prosecco people. Whenever we get together, whether it's for a holiday or something much less celebratory, way too much prosecco is always involved. Straight-up is an excellent option, of course, but paired with the seasonal flavors of cranberry, ginger, and rosemary, prosecco becomes Christmas in a cup.

In a small pot over medium-low heat, combine the sugar, rosemary, and ginger with ¾ cup of water and bring the mixture to a simmer. Allow the mixture to bubble away for 20 minutes, stirring occasionally, in order to dissolve the sugar and infuse the syrup with the rosemary and ginger. Strain this simple syrup through a fine mesh sieve into a bowl and place it in the fridge to chill completely.

To make a cocktail, combine 2 tablespoons of the ginger rosemary syrup with 3 tablespoons of the cranberry juice in a champagne flute and top it all off with chilled prosecco. Garnish with a few frozen cranberries and small sprig of rosemary.

Cheddar Popovers

MAKES 12

1 cup buttermilk or whole milk
2 eggs
1 cup all-purpose flour
1 teaspoon kosher salt
¼ cup unsalted butter
1 cup cubed extra-old white cheddar cheese

Cheddar popovers are essentially cheese pillows for your plate. Need I say more?

Place a 12-cup muffin or popover pan on the middle rack of your oven and preheat the oven to 450°F.

In a large glass measuring cup, measure out the buttermilk (or milk) and whisk in the eggs. Whisk in the flour and salt and set aside.

When the oven has reached temperature, remove the pan and place about 1 teaspoon of butter into each well. Place the pan back in the oven for about 2 minutes to melt the butter. Remove the pan from the oven and pour about ¼ cup of batter into each well. This should fill the wells a little over halfway. Divide the cheese among the soon-to-be popovers and bake for 20 minutes.

Without opening the oven, turn down the heat to 350°F and bake for another 15 to 20 minutes, or until the popovers are perfectly puffy and golden brown.

Serve immediately for best flavor, but to be honest, they are still pretty stinking amazing reheated in a hot oven for a few minutes just before you sit down to your Christmas feast.

Pancetta-Wrapped Turkey Roulade

SERVES 8

6–7 cups torn stuffing bread or challah
¼ cup unsalted butter
1½ cups diced cooking onion
1½ cups diced celery
Kosher salt
Freshly ground black pepper
½ cup dried cranberries, chopped
3 tablespoons finely chopped fresh sage leaves, divided
1½ tablespoons finely chopped fresh rosemary leaves, divided
1½ tablespoons finely chopped fresh thyme leaves, divided
¼ cup brandy
1 cup chopped pecans
1½–2 cups no- or low-sodium chicken broth
1 egg, lightly beaten
5½–6½ oz boneless, skinless turkey breasts, about 3 breasts
10½–12½ oz thinly sliced pancetta, about 50 slices

I've always been a fan of gift wrap rather than gift bags stuffed with tissue paper, and I feel that rolling a roast in a thin layer of pancetta is like wrapping an edible gift for your Christmas table. Not only does it give your dinner an automatic celebratory feel, it also helps seal in all the flavor and, as all the fats render out of the pancetta, it saves you the trouble of basting.

The night before you are going to assemble your roulade, prepare the stuffing bread by laying the bread bits on a baking sheet in an even single layer and allowing them to get stale overnight.

The next day, melt the butter in a large, deep pot over medium-low heat and sauté the onions and celery until tender and slightly translucent, about 3 to 4 minutes. Season with salt and pepper and add in the dried cranberries, 2 tablespoons of the sage, 1½ teaspoons of the rosemary, and 1½ teaspoons of the thyme. Add in the brandy and stir until all of the liquid has evaporated. Remove the pot from the heat and fold in the stale bread and pecans. Mix well, taste and adjust seasonings to your preference, and allow to cool slightly.

In a small bowl, whisk together 1 cup of the broth with the egg and add to the cooled stuffing mixture. If the mixture looks a little dry, add a splash more broth. Set the stuffing aside while you get to work on your turkey.

Place 1 breast on a large, sturdy cutting board with the pointed, thinner end toward you and the underside of the breast facing up. Holding a sharp knife parallel to the board, slice sideways into the thickest part of the breast about halfway down horizontally. Cut along the length of the breast, almost to the edge but being careful not to cut all the way through. Open and flatten the butterflied turkey breast so that it is now wider and relatively even in thickness. Set this aside and repeat with the other breasts.

Line a large cutting board with plastic wrap and place long pieces of kitchen twine about 2 inches apart horizontally along the board. Place the pancetta in an overlapping layer over the twine and plastic wrap. Aim for a square of pancetta slices about 7 pieces long and 7 pieces wide. Scatter the remaining sage, rosemary, and thyme evenly over top

of the pancetta, and season with salt and pepper. Lay your butterflied turkey breasts over the pancetta, cut side up, almost like a puzzle, so that you have a solid layer of turkey. Trim off any extra bits of turkey, making sure to fill in the gaps.

Season the turkey with salt and pepper and spoon an even layer of stuffing over the meat. Using the plastic wrap to assist you, roll the turkey and pancetta up into a cylinder and tie the twine to secure the roulade into a compact roast. Tightly seal the plastic wrap around the roast.

To roast, preheat your oven to 325°F and line a baking sheet or roasting pan with a wire rack. Place the roulade on the rack and, using the plastic wrap to help, unroll the plastic so that the roast lands seam side down. Discard the plastic wrap and roast the roulade for 1½ to 2 hours, or until a thermometer inserted in the center of the turkey registers 150°F. The outside of the turkey will have reached 165°F by this point.

Remove the roulade from the oven and cover loosely with aluminum foil. Allow the roast to rest for 15 to 20 minutes before slicing and serving with all the trimmings.

Notes:

1. The roulade can be prepared up to 1 day in advance. Just place the uncooked wrapped roulade on a baking sheet and store it in the fridge. Before roasting, allow it to sit at room temperature for about 30 minutes.

2. Stuffing bread is basically just white sandwich bread infused with sage and poultry seasoning. It is a Berg family staple, but if you can't find it, challah also works wonderfully. Any leftover stuffing can go into a small buttered baking dish to be baked alongside the turkey for the last 30 minutes or so, until golden on top and cooked through.

Cranberry Sage Sauce

MAKES ABOUT 2 ½ CUPS

- 1 (12 oz) bag fresh cranberries (or 3 cups frozen, thawed)
- 1 cup granulated sugar
- 2 whole star anise
- 1 sprig sage
- 1 tablespoon grainy Dijon mustard
- ½ teaspoon fine sea salt
- ½ teaspoon freshly ground black pepper

Cranberry sauce is the simplest thing in the world. I'd even argue that wrestling with a can opener is more difficult than making this recipe so, in my opinion, a big bowl of homemade crans should always make its way onto your holiday table. For this slightly savory version, I've added sage, pepper, star anise, and a little grainy Dijon to help those tart little berries sing.

Combine the cranberries, sugar, star anise, and sage with 1 cup of water in a medium pot over medium heat and bring the mixture to a simmer. Allow it to bubble away until the berries begin to pop and get a little jammy, about 10 to 15 minutes.

Remove the cranberries from the heat, fish out the star anise and sage, and, using the back of a spoon, mash some of the berries against the side of the pot. Season with the Dijon, salt, and pepper, and allow to cool before storing in the fridge in a tightly covered container.

Note:
If you're looking to get ahead, the cranberry sauce will keep in your fridge for up to 2 weeks or in your freezer for up to 3 months.

Secret Ingredient Mashed Potatoes

SERVES 8 BERGS/FOOTES (AKA 10-12 NORMAL PEOPLE)

- 6 lb yellow potatoes, peeled and quartered
- 1 cup milk
- 1 cup whipping (35%) cream
- 1 head roasted garlic (see note)
- ¾ cup unsalted butter
- ½ cup buttermilk
- 2-4 tablespoons prepared horseradish
- 2-3 teaspoons kosher salt

My family is pretty serious about potatoes. The basic estimate when prepping for a Berg/Foote party is about 2 pounds per person—no joke. We'll eat them any which way, but this is my personal favorite. Roasted garlic, horseradish, and buttermilk freshen up classic mashers just in time for the holidays.

Place the peeled and quartered potatoes in a large pot and cover with cool tap water. Season with salt and bring to a boil over high heat. Cook the potatoes until fork-tender, about 15 to 20 minutes.

Meanwhile, heat the milk and cream in a clean pot over low heat and mash in the full head of roasted garlic.

When the potatoes are tender, drain them well and return them to the pot. Using a handheld masher, mash the potatoes until creamy. Then, if you like them nice and smooth, switch to an electric handheld mixer. Add in the hot garlicky milk, butter, and buttermilk, and whip to combine. Stir in 2 tablespoons of the horseradish and season with salt. Give the potatoes a taste and see if they need any more horseradish or salt.

Keep the potatoes in the pot, covered, over very low heat until you're ready to serve.

Note:

To roast garlic, remove any loose papery layers from the garlic bulb and trim about ¼ inch from the top to expose the cloves. Place the bulb on a piece of aluminum foil, drizzle with 1 teaspoon of olive oil, and wrap the foil around the garlic. Roast in a 400°F oven for 25 minutes, or until the garlic is soft and golden. To use, squeeze the garlic from each clove.

Bacon Hazelnut Green Beans

SERVES 8–10

2 lb green beans, ends trimmed
½ cup hazelnuts, coarsely chopped
4 slices thick-cut bacon, diced
1 tablespoon sherry vinegar
2 teaspoons liquid honey
Kosher salt
Freshly ground black pepper

The one and only Myra Berg hates two things: pink food and green beans. She claims the former just shouldn't exist and the latter are too squeaky to be enjoyable. I always counter this with the fact that she loves cheese curds, the world's squeakiest food, but there is no reasoning with my mom once she's made up her mind. That is, until I made her these.

Steam the green beans just until tender but still a wee bit crisp, about 4 to 5 minutes.

Meanwhile, toast the hazelnuts in a large stainless steel frying pan over medium heat until fragrant and just starting to brown, about 1 to 2 minutes. Transfer the toasted nuts to a plate and set aside. Place the frying pan back over the heat and add in the bacon. Cook until crisp, about 6 to 8 minutes, and then deglaze the pan with the vinegar and stir in the honey. Add the beans and the hazelnuts, and season with salt and pepper. Give everything a good toss to coat and serve.

Note:
To get ahead, blanch the green beans and toast the hazelnuts a few hours in advance. Keep the green beans in the fridge until ready to toss and reheat with the sweet bacon-y drippings.

Cheesy Baked Onions

SERVES 8

- 8–12 cooking onions, trimmed and peeled
- 1 teaspoon kosher salt
- ½ teaspoon freshly cracked black pepper
- ⅛ teaspoon freshly grated nutmeg
- 1 cup whipping (35%) cream
- 1 cup grated Gruyère or Emmental cheese
- ½ cup grated Parmigiano-Reggiano cheese

When the Christmas table is groaning under 73 pounds of mashed potatoes, a glorious bird, vats of gravy, and all of the fixings, everyone in my family reaches for these first. The spiciness of the yellow cooking onions slowly cooks away, leaving you with a big dish of mellow, sweet, and tender bulbs. Topped with golden, bubbling cheese and drowned in heavy cream, even the most allium-averse will be hooked.

Preheat your oven to 350°F, lightly grease a 9-inch square or 10-inch round casserole dish, and set a pot of salted water to boil over high heat.

Cook the onions in the boiling salted water for 10–15 minutes, or until a sharp knife can easily pierce the center. Remove them from the water, quarter them through the root, and place them cut side up in the prepared dish. Season with the salt, pepper, and nutmeg and pour the cream over top. Scatter both cheeses over top and bake for 20 to 25 minutes, or until the cheese is browned.

Note:

You can't cut corners when it comes to the cream in this recipe. If you use anything other than whipping cream, the dairy will split. But this is Christmas and everyone knows that calories don't count at Christmas.

LEFT: GREEN BEANS (PAGE 188)

RIGHT: CHEESY BAKED ONIONS (PAGE 189)

Mom's So-Called "Famous" Cheesecake

MAKES 1 (9-INCH) CHEESECAKE

½ cup graham cracker crumbs
2 cups creamed cottage cheese
2 cups brick-style cream cheese
1½ cups granulated sugar
¼ cup cornstarch
4 eggs
½ cup unsalted butter, melted
2 tablespoons lemon juice
2 teaspoons pure vanilla extract
½ cup raspberry jelly
2 cups fresh berries

Note:
If your food processor's capacity is less than 11 cups, process the cottage cheese and cream cheese together and then transfer them to your stand mixer to incorporate the remaining ingredients.

Never in all my years on this earth have I ever seen my mom come even close to making anything resembling a cheesecake. For the past six years or so, I've asked for her mythical cheesecake for my birthday dessert, but low and behold, something always comes up. It's become our family's very own white whale. But, hey, the recipe she's passed down to me is pretty darn tasty, so I guess she's forgiven. With no real crust and the odd addition of cottage cheese, this recipe is just as strange and wonderful as my very own Mama B.

Preheat your oven to 325°F, grease a 9-inch springform pan with butter or cooking spray, and wrap the outside of the pan very well with aluminum foil.

Sprinkle the graham cracker crumbs into the pan and shake it around to lightly coat the bottom and sides, then set aside. Boil a kettle of water while you prepare your filling.

Place both cheeses in a food processor fitted with the steel blade and process until very smooth, about 1 minute, being sure to scrape down the bowl once or twice. In a small bowl, combine the sugar and cornstarch. With the mixer running, gradually add the sugar mixture into the cheese. Add in the eggs, one at a time. Drizzle in the butter, lemon juice, and vanilla and continue to mix just until you have a creamy filling.

Pour the cheesecake mixture into your prepared pan and place the cheesecake into a larger high-sided pan, such as a roasting pan. Pour the hot water from the kettle into the larger pan so that it comes about 1 inch up the side of the cheesecake pan and bake for 1 hour and 10 minutes. Without opening the oven door, turn off the oven and allow the cake to cool in the oven for 1½ to 2 hours. Place the cheesecake, uncovered, in the fridge for at least 4 hours to firm up.

To serve, warm the raspberry jelly in the microwave for 15 to 30 seconds, or until slightly liquefied. Toss the berries in the warmed jelly and spoon over the chilled cheesecake.

BOTTOM LEFT OF IMAGE: BELLINI (PAGE 177)

Laid-Back New Year's Feast

Nothing spells New Year's Eve quite like fondue, tourtière, and too much bubbly. Taking a cue from kitchen goddess Ina Garten, I like to whip up a New Year's feast that is simple, homey, and classic, with a few twists.

Even though this is a laid-back feast, the cocktail and dessert are complete showstoppers. It *is* New Year's Eve, after all.

Aperol Sorbet Spritz

MAKES ABOUT 2 QUARTS OF SORBET
(AKA ENOUGH FOR A WHOLE BUNCH OF COCKTAILS)

1¾ cups granulated sugar
½ cup Aperol
½ cup orange juice
1 tablespoon grated orange zest
As many bottles of prosecco as you can carry

I am always down for an Aperol Spritz. The color, the bubbles, the little bit of bitter from that strange Italian elixir—how can you go wrong?! Think of this as an adult ice cream float; just replace the super-sweet root beer with prosecco and plain Jane vanilla ice cream with homemade Aperol sorbet.

In a medium pot over medium-high heat, place the sugar in 2½ cups water, bring to a simmer, and cook for 10 minutes, or until all of the sugar has dissolved, stirring occasionally. Remove from the heat and allow this simple syrup to cool to room temperature. Add in the Aperol, orange juice, and orange zest and refrigerate for at least 4 hours to chill completely.

Freeze this mixture in your ice cream maker according to the manufacturer's instructions, then transfer to a container. Freeze until solid.

To serve, scoop about 2 heaping tablespoons of the sorbet into a coupe glass and top with prosecco.

Note:
If you don't have an ice cream maker, fret not! Simply pour the chilled mixture into a 9- x 13-inch pan. Freeze for 30 to 40 minutes, until icy around the edges. Give the mixture a stir and repeat the freezing/stirring process until the mixture is fully frozen. When you're ready to serve, use a fork to scrape off the top of what is now a granita. Place it in a glass and top with some bubbly.

Herbed Mushroom and Camembert Skillet

SERVES 8

- 2 tablespoons unsalted butter
- 1 tablespoon olive oil
- 3–4 cups assorted mushrooms, cleaned, sliced or torn (see note)
- 1 sprig rosemary
- 3 sprigs thyme
- Kosher salt
- Freshly cracked black pepper
- 1 clove garlic, finely minced
- ¼ cup dry white wine
- 8½–10½ oz Camembert cheese, cubed
- Crusty French bread

When I was little, my mom used to invite all of our neighbors over for a New Year's Eve fondue party. There'd be a few pots bubbling away with Gruyère, a couple filled with hot oil surrounded by steak, chicken, and shrimp, and, of course, some silky chocolate fondue for dessert. Rather than make you go to all of the trouble of setting up a fondue pot and carefully adding cheese to bubbling white wine, I offer you my cheater's version.

Position an oven rack in the top third of your oven and turn on the broiler.

Set a cast iron, or other ovenproof, skillet over medium-high heat and melt the butter and oil. Toss in the mushrooms, rosemary, and thyme and season with a little salt and pepper. Cook the mushrooms until they have released their liquid and all of it has evaporated and the mushrooms begin to caramelize, about 5 to 6 minutes. Turn off the heat and add in first the garlic and then the white wine. Stir, scraping the bottom of the pan to deglaze, until all of the wine has evaporated.

Scatter the cheese on top of the mushrooms and place the pan in the oven. Broil for 3 to 5 minutes, or until the cheese is melted and bubbling. Serve hot from the oven with lots of crusty bread for dipping.

Note:

Any mushrooms or combo of mushrooms would be delicious, but shiitake, Portobello, cremini, and king oyster are my favorites for this recipe.

Maple-Glazed Parsnips

SERVES 8–10

- 12–15 medium parsnips, peeled and cut into 2-inch chunks
- 2 tablespoons extra virgin olive oil
- 1 teaspoon kosher salt
- ½ teaspoon freshly ground black pepper
- ⅛ teaspoon freshly grated nutmeg
- 2 tablespoons unsalted butter
- 3 tablespoons pure maple syrup

Parsnips are like the candy of the root vegetable world. Roasted with a little olive oil, lots of black pepper, a pinch of nutmeg, and a glug of maple syrup, they're the sweetest little tuber to ever grace your table.

Preheat your oven to 375°F and line a baking sheet with aluminum foil. Place the parsnips on the baking sheet, drizzle with the oil, and season with the salt, pepper, and nutmeg. Dot the butter over the parsnips and roast for 20 minutes. Drizzle the maple syrup over top, roll the parsnips around a bit, and roast for another 15 to 20 minutes, or until golden brown and tender.

Mashed Butternut Squash with Crispy Sage

SERVES 8

- 2 cups pure carrot juice
- 2 teaspoons cornstarch
- 2 butternut squashes, peeled, seeded, and cubed
- ¼ cup unsalted butter, melted
- 2 teaspoons kosher salt
- ¼ teaspoon freshly ground black pepper
- ¼ teaspoon freshly grated nutmeg
- 2 tablespoons vegetable oil
- 8–12 sage leaves

My secret ingredient for any mashed orange veg is carrot juice. In this recipe, when it's reduced to about half its original volume, it lends the most wonderful silky sweetness to your mash and, combined with the crispy sage, takes this dish to the next level.

Pour 1 tablespoon of the carrot juice into a small bowl and place the rest in a medium pot. Simmer the juice over medium heat for about 20 minutes, or until reduced by half. Whisk the cornstarch into the reserved cold carrot juice and whisk this mix into the reduced carrot juice. Continue to simmer, whisking, for a few minutes, until thickened.

Meanwhile, boil the squashes in a large pot until fork-tender, about 15 to 20 minutes. Drain the squashes, return them to the pot, and mash with a potato masher. Using an electric handheld mixer, whip the squashes with the carrot juice, butter, salt, pepper, and nutmeg. Place a lid on the pot and keep the squash warm over very low heat while you fry your sage.

For the sage, heat the oil in a small frying pan over medium heat. Fry the sage for a few seconds per side until crisp, then transfer to a piece of paper towel to drain, and season with a bit of salt.

Serve the butternut squash topped with the crispy sage.

Tourtière

SERVES 8–10

FOR THE FILLING

2 teaspoons vegetable oil
2 small cooking onions, diced
1–2 cloves garlic, minced
2 bay leaves
2 teaspoons kosher salt
1¼ lb lean ground beef
1¼ lb ground pork
1 large russet potato, peeled and grated
2 teaspoons unsalted butter
2 tablespoons all-purpose flour
½ cup stout or hearty red wine
1¼–1½ cups no- or low-sodium beef broth
8–10 dashes Worcestershire sauce
1 teaspoon herbes de Provence
½ teaspoon ground cinnamon
¼ teaspoon ground cloves
⅛ teaspoon freshly grated nutmeg
½ teaspoon freshly ground black pepper

FOR THE PASTRY

1 cup unsalted butter, cubed
3¾ cups all-purpose flour
1 teaspoon kosher salt
1 egg + 2 teaspoons milk, for egg wash

Tourtière is a Quebecois holiday classic that I love to serve on New Year's Eve (rather than Christmas Eve). It's unpretentious, hearty enough to help you handle some drinks later, and so good cold from the fridge as a late-night snack. Plus, if your New Year's resolution is to find the perfect pastry for a meat pie, look no further than this hot water pastry!

For the filling, heat the oil in a large frying pan over medium heat and sauté the onions, garlic, and bay leaves for about 2 minutes, or until slightly translucent. Season with the salt and add in the beef and pork. Cook for 10 minutes and then add in the potato and butter. Stir to combine and melt the butter, and then sprinkle the flour over top. Give it all a stir and cook for 2 minutes in order to cook off that raw flour taste. Still stirring, pour in the stout (or wine) and broth. Season with the Worcestershire, herbes de Provence, cinnamon, cloves, and nutmeg, and finish it all off with the pepper. Cook for 5 minutes to bring everything together. Remove the filling from the heat and allow it to cool to room temperature.

Meanwhile, make the hot water pastry by combining the butter with 1 cup of water in a large pot over medium-high heat. Bring this to a boil and, once all of the butter has melted, remove it from the heat and dump in the flour and salt. Working quickly, stir well until everything comes together and then turn the dough out onto a lightly floured work surface. When it's cool enough to handle, knead the dough until very smooth and a little elastic. Don't be shy here—I often knead this dough for at least 3 minutes and the result is somehow better than if I'd been gentle with it. Allow the dough to rest at room temperature, lightly covered with plastic wrap, for about 30 minutes.

Preheat your oven to 400°F and divide your dough into two chunks, one slightly larger than the other. Roll the larger piece out on a lightly floured work surface so that it's big enough to line the base and sides of a 9-inch springform pan. Line the pan with the dough, spoon in the filling, and roll out the remaining piece of dough. Top the pie with this piece of dough, crimp the edges, and cut a few slits in the middle of the tourtière to create a steam vent. Brush with the egg wash and place on a baking sheet to catch any overflow. Bake for 25 minutes, turn down the

oven to 350°F, and continue baking for 30 to 35 minutes, or until the crust is golden. Allow the tourtière to rest for at least 10 minutes before slicing and serving.

Note:

This tourtière can be assembled up to 1 day ahead and stored, tightly covered, in the fridge. When you're ready to serve, remove the tourtière from the fridge to let it sit while you preheat the oven, and bake as above.

RIGHT: SWISS ROLL (PAGE 204)

LEFT: TOURTIÈRE (PAGE 200), MAPLE-GLAZED PARSNIPS (PAGE 198) AND MASHED BUTTERNUT SQUASH (PAGE 199)

Bubbly Swiss Roll with Kir Royale Buttercream

MAKES 1 (10-INCH-LONG) SWISS ROLL

FOR THE CAKE

- 4 eggs, separated
- 1⁄4 teaspoon cream of tartar
- 3⁄4 cup granulated sugar, divided
- 2 tablespoons buttermilk
- 1 teaspoon pure vanilla extract
- 1⁄4 cup cava or prosecco
- 1 1⁄4 cups cake and pastry flour
- 1 teaspoon baking powder
- 1⁄2 teaspoon fine sea salt
- 6 drops red food coloring

FOR THE KIR ROYALE BUTTERCREAM

- 1⁄2 cup unsalted butter
- 3 cups icing sugar
- 2 tablespoons cava or prosecco
- 2 teaspoons crème de cassis or blackcurrant cordial, such as Ribena
- 1 teaspoon pure vanilla extract
- 1⁄4 teaspoon fine sea salt
- 4–6 drops red food coloring

FOR THE ASSEMBLY:

- 1⁄2 cup red currant jam
- 1⁄4 cup icing sugar

My friend Veronica is the queen of roll cakes. When she casually whipped up a matcha chestnut Japanese roll cake in the MasterChef Canada kitchen, everyone was in awe. Seriously, it was bonkers. She made a whole cake in under an hour without a recipe and it was the most beautiful thing I've ever seen. Well, Veronica, here is my attempt at a showstopping roll cake. Infused with the flavors of New Year's Eve and decorated at the batter level in true Veronica Cham fashion, it's the perfect end to any New Year's feast.

Preheat your oven to 350°F and spray a 10- × 15-inch jelly roll pan with cooking spray. Line the bottom of the pan with parchment paper and set aside. Make sure the bowl and whisk attachment for your stand mixer are squeaky clean and get to work on your cake.

Separate your eggs. Place the whites in the bowl of your stand mixer and the yolks into a small bowl. Add the cream of tartar to the egg whites and whip on high until soft peaks form, about 1 to 2 minutes. Gradually sprinkle in 1⁄4 cup of the sugar and continue to whip until the egg whites reach stiff peaks, about 3 to 4 minutes. Transfer them a separate bowl and place the yolks in the mixer with the remaining sugar, the buttermilk, and vanilla. Whip on high for 2 to 3 minutes, or until the yolks are lighter in color and almost doubled in volume. With the machine running, drizzle in the sparkling wine and continue whipping to combine. Remove the bowl from the mixer and sift the flour, baking powder, and salt over the yolk mixture. Gently fold everything until almost fully combined. Fold in about one-third of the whipped whites until almost combined. Add in the remaining whites and fold just until combined.

Scoop a hefty 1⁄4 cup of the batter into a small bowl and stir in the red food coloring. Using a spoon, gently drizzle or drop little polka dots of the pink batter onto your prepared baking sheet in any pattern you'd like. Place this in the oven for 2 to 3 minutes, just to set the batter. Remove the pan from the oven and gently spoon the remaining white batter over the design. Spread the batter out so that it reaches all sides of the pan in an even layer and bake for 14 to 17 minutes, or until the cake is cooked and springs back when you touch it.

Allow the cake to cool in the pan for 3 minutes and then run a metal spatula around the edges of the pan to loosen it. Invert the cake onto a wire rack, remove the parchment, and dust the cake with some icing sugar to help prevent it from sticking. Place a clean kitchen towel over the cake and invert it once again so that it's pattern side down. Dust this side with some icing sugar as well and then, starting at the short end of the cake, roll it up into a jelly roll, folding the towel in on the cake as you go. Allow the cake to cool to room temperature for about 1 hour.

Meanwhile, make the buttercream by beating the butter with the icing sugar in your stand mixer, fitted with a paddle attachment. Add in the sparkling wine, cordial, vanilla, salt, and food coloring. Beat on medium speed until light and creamy, about 1 to 2 minutes.

To assemble, gently unroll the cake onto a cutting board, pattern side down. Evenly spread the jam over it, followed by the Kir Royale buttercream. Reroll the cake, plate, and give it a little sprinkle of icing sugar just before serving.

Holiday Hangover Brunch

Whether it's Boxing Day, New Year's Day, or just the morning after a big family party, fuzzy heads and rumbly tummies are pretty much a given. My remedy for this is a good old-fashioned Canadian Fry-Up. Inspired by the classic English breakfast feast of sausage, back bacon, beans, tomatoes, fried bread, and eggs, if this doesn't cure your hangover, I don't know what will. Just be sure to have lots of strong coffee on hand.

Canadian Baked Beans

SERVES 8

2 cups dried navy beans, soaked overnight at room temperature
1 cup barbeque sauce
¼ cup pure maple syrup
2 tablespoons smooth Dijon mustard
1 tablespoon tomato paste
1 teaspoon freshly ground black pepper
3 strips smoky bacon (optional)
2 teaspoons kosher salt

Classic tomato-y baked beans are a staple in an English breakfast, but for this Canadian Fry-Up, I've gone the maple route. They take a bit of time in a slow cooker, so whip them up a day or two before you expect to encounter a fuzzy morning.

Place the soaked navy beans in your slow cooker and add in 3 cups of cold water, the barbeque sauce, maple syrup, Dijon, tomato paste, pepper, and finally the bacon (if using). Stir well to combine, place the lid on the slow cooker, and cook on low for 6 to 7 hours, or until the beans are tender.

Once the beans are cooked, stir in the salt and place the beans in the fridge overnight to allow the flavors to meld and the starches to develop.

To serve, return the beans to the slow cooker to heat, or reheat in a pot over medium heat.

Maple Peameal Bacon Roast

SERVES 8–10

- 2½–2¾ lb peameal bacon roast
- ¼ cup yellow cornmeal, plus more for sprinkling
- ¼–½ cup pure maple syrup
- 1 teaspoon freshly ground black pepper
- ¼ teaspoon kosher salt

How could I have a Canadian breakfast without Canadian bacon? Smothering it in maple syrup pushes this little piggy into a whole new realm of deliciousness. To make life extra simple if you're feeding a crowd, this bacon is prepared as a roast to be carved at the table so that all of your guests can help themselves. Any leftovers are amazing the next day in a classic peameal sandwich.

Preheat your oven to 375°F and line a baking sheet or roasting pan with a wire rack.

Sprinkle your peameal with the cornmeal and cut a crosshatch pattern about ½-inch deep into the fatty topside of the roast. Using a pastry brush, daub the top and all four sides of the roast with the maple syrup and season with the pepper and salt.

Cook the roast in the oven, uncovered, for 1 hour. Cover it loosely with aluminum foil and cook for another 35 to 45 minutes, or until the internal temperature reaches 155°F to 160°F.

Allow the roast to rest, tented with the aluminum foil, for about 10 to 15 minutes before serving.

OPPOSITE:
BAKED BEANS (PAGE 207),
BANNOCK (PAGE 210),
EGGS EN COCOTTE (PAGE 211)

Whole Wheat Cheddar Bannock

MAKES 12

1½ cups whole wheat flour
1½ cups all-purpose flour
2½ tablespoons baking powder
2 teaspoons kosher salt
1¼ cups grated extra-old white cheddar cheese
¼ cup unsalted butter, melted
2 teaspoons liquid honey
Vegetable oil, for cooking

Bannock is kind of the perfect cross between a biscuit, a pancake, and an English muffin. It's amazing fresh out of the frying pan, smeared with lots of butter, as part of a Canadian Fry-Up.

In a large bowl, combine both flours with the baking powder and salt. Mix in the cheese. In a separate bowl, whisk 1½ cups of warm water with the butter and honey. Pour this liquid into the dry ingredients. Stir with a wooden spoon just until a loose dough forms. If the dough seems dry, add another few tablespoons of water.

Dump the dough out onto a work surface dusted with flour, and dust the top of the dough with a little more flour. Using your hands, press the dough down to about a ½-inch thickness and fold it over onto itself. Repeat this patting and folding three or four times, then shape the dough into a rough rectangle. Using a knife or a pastry cutter, divide it into 12 evenly sized biscuit-y portions and get ready to fry!

Heat a cast iron skillet or frying pan over medium heat and add enough oil to thinly coat the bottom of the pan. When the oil is hot, fry the bannock, in batches, for about 3 to 4 minutes per side, or until deep golden brown. If your pan starts to look a little dry, add a bit more oil and allow it to heat up again before frying more bannock.

Note:
As with bread dough, biscuit and bannock dough may require a little extra flour on humid days. If the dough seems sticky, add a few more tablespoons of flour until it's a manageable consistency.

Eggs en Cocotte

SERVES 8

- 2 tablespoons unsalted butter
- 3 cloves garlic, finely minced
- 1 shallot, finely minced
- 2–3 large handfuls baby spinach
- 4 tablespoons finely chopped fresh chives, divided
- 4 tablespoons finely chopped flat-leaf parsley, divided
- Kosher salt
- Freshly ground black pepper
- 16 eggs
- ¼ cup whipping (35%) cream
- ½ cup finely grated Parmigiano-Reggiano cheese

Confession: I really only like my eggs baked, poached, or boiled. Don't get me wrong, I'll eat a fried egg, and I've been known to indulge in a scramble or two if it's smothered in cheese, but baked, poached, and boiled are the eggs that have a real place in my heart. Not only do I prefer their taste, but when they're prepared in any of these ways, they are pretty darn easy to make for a crowd. On a day like New Year's Day, when brains might be fuzzy and tummies grumbly, these eggs are the way to go.

Preheat your oven to 350°F and lightly grease eight small ramekins or ovenproof dishes. Place the ramekins on a baking sheet and set aside.

In a frying pan over medium-low heat, melt the butter and cook the garlic and shallots until sweated and fragrant, about 2 minutes. Remove the pan from the heat and stir in the spinach with 3 tablespoons each of the chives and parsley. Wilt the spinach, about 3 to 5 minutes. Season the spinach mixture with salt and pepper and divide it between the prepared ramekins. Crack 2 eggs into each ramekin and top with about 1½ teaspoons of whipping cream followed by 1 tablespoon of cheese.

Bake the eggs for 16 to 20 minutes, depending on how you like your yolks—16 minutes will give you runny yolks and 20 will be closer to medium. Remove the eggs from the oven, garnish with the remaining chives and parsley, and season with a sprinkling of salt and pepper. The whites will not be completely set, but when you start mixing everything up with toast and such, it will come together beautifully.

Summer Savory Grilled Tomatoes

SERVES 8

- 8 tomatoes on the vine, cored, halved crosswise, and juicy pulp removed
- 2 cloves garlic, minced
- 2 tablespoons finely chopped flat-leaf parsley
- 1 teaspoon dried summer savory (see note)
- Kosher salt
- Freshly ground black pepper
- 1 tablespoon extra virgin olive oil
- 2 tablespoons unsalted butter
- 6 tablespoons panko crumbs

An integral part of any proper Canadian (*cough* English *cough*) breakfast, the humble tomato lends acidity and freshness to a plate that can often seem very "cooked." The addition of summer savory brings a welcome East Coast flavor to these tomatoes—and don't worry, there is no need to pull out the barbeque. The tomatoes aren't grilled in the North American sense but rather in the classic British way. That is, broiled.

Position an oven rack in the center of your oven and preheat your oven to 350°F.

Place the tomatoes, cut side up, in a baking dish just large enough to hold them and scatter each one evenly with garlic, parsley, and summer savory. Season with salt and pepper and drizzle with the oil.

In a small frying pan over medium heat, melt the butter and then stir in the panko crumbs. Season with salt and pepper and allow the panko to toast for about 30 seconds.

Divide the panko over top the tomatoes and place the dish in the oven for 15 minutes. Turn on the broiler and broil the tomatoes, still on the center rack, for 2 to 4 minutes, or until golden. Serve warm.

Note:
If dry summer savory is not available, dried regular savory or thyme are good substitutes.

**Can easily be shared between non-romantically involved pairs*

Party of Two

FOR THE ROMANTICS* IN THE CROWD

Just a Regular Tuesday

No matter the day, no matter the meal, Aaron digs into anything I make him like it's the best thing he's ever eaten. I can't wait to eat all of my Tuesday-night dinners sitting across the table from this guy forever and always.

Shrimp Cardinale and Grits

SERVES 2 WITH LEFTOVERS

FOR THE SHRIMP

1 lb uncooked shrimp, peeled and deveined
½ teaspoon cayenne pepper
1 lemon, quartered
3 slices thick-cut bacon, diced
1½ tablespoons unsalted butter
½ medium cooking onion, diced
1 green bell pepper, diced
2 cloves garlic, minced
1 cup diced tomatoes, with their juices
1 tablespoon tomato paste
½ teaspoon smoked paprika
1 tablespoon all-purpose flour
¼ cup dry white wine
½ cup no- or low-sodium chicken or vegetable broth
½ teaspoon Worcestershire sauce
4–5 dashes Tabasco sauce
½ cup chopped flat-leaf parsley
Kosher salt
Freshly ground black pepper

FOR THE GRITS

1½ cups milk
1 teaspoon kosher salt
½ teaspoon freshly ground black pepper
1 cup stoneground grits
3 tablespoons unsalted butter
1½ cups shredded white cheddar cheese

Southern cuisine has such a strong influence on the way I cook. I trace it all back to family vacations down on Kiawah Island, South Carolina. We would all pile into the car, with my dad's fishing and crabbing gear in tow, for the 17-hour trek, and within about five minutes of arriving, we'd be running down to the beach or over to the salt flats, avoiding 'gators all the way. Whenever I'm stuck on what to make on a casual Tuesday night for Aaron and me, I know that I can always fall back on those Southern flavors. This is my take on the Low Country classic, with a little bit of Creole influence.

For the shrimp, arrange them in a dish large enough to hold them without crowding and season with the cayenne pepper and the juice from one lemon quarter. Place the shrimp in the fridge to marinate while you prepare the sauce and grits.

In a large frying pan or deep-sided pot over medium heat, cook the bacon until crisp. Transfer it to a plate and add the butter, then the onion and bell pepper, to the bacon fat in the pan. Cook for about 4 to 5 minutes, or until fragrant and sweating, then add in the garlic and tomatoes with their juices and cook for 3 to 4 minutes. Stir in the tomato paste and paprika, then sprinkle the flour over top and give everything a good stir. Allow this to cook for 3 to 4 more minutes, then deglaze the pan with the white wine.

Add in the broth and Worcestershire and Tabasco sauces and cook down until thickened, about 10 minutes. Once it's thick, turn down the heat to low, cover the pot, and get to work on your grits.

For the grits, place the milk, salt, and pepper in a large pot over medium-high heat. Add in 2½ cups of water and bring to a boil. Once it's boiling, start whisking. While whisking, slowly pour in the grits. Turn down the heat to low, cover the pot, and cook for 15 minutes. Give the grits a stir and then replace the lid and cook for another 5 to 10 minutes, or until creamy. Remove the pot from the heat, stir in the butter, followed by the cheese, and cover to keep warm.

CONTINUES

TOP LEFT OF IMAGE:

BUTTERMILK BISCUITS (PAGE 220)

Grab the shrimp from the fridge and add them, along with the bacon, to the sauce. Cook just until the shrimp are pretty and pink, about 3 to 4 minutes.

Stir in the parsley and squeeze a lemon quarter over top. Season with salt and pepper to taste and, if you're like me, add in a bit more hot sauce and lemon juice.

Serve the shrimp over the cheesy grits with the remaining lemon quarters on the side and get ready to mosey on down South!

Buttermilk Biscuits

MAKES 10–12

2 cups all-purpose flour
1½ tablespoons baking powder
¼ teaspoon baking soda
1 teaspoon kosher salt
¼ cup unsalted butter, straight from the fridge
1¼–1½ cups buttermilk, straight from the fridge
2 tablespoons unsalted butter, melted

Note:
This recipe makes more than enough biscuits for two but, believe me, that's a good thing. They are ridiculously good, so you're definitely going to want a few straight out of the oven, and they are perfect toasted in the morning for breakfast.

Every single person in the world loves a good biscuit. Seriously, I've yet to meet anyone I can't win over with these fluffy, humble, buttery guys. They're addictive fresh out of the oven and slathered with butter or served next to something extra saucy. This is one of those recipes that gets better the more often you make it, so step to it! After all, shrimp and grits ain't shrimp and grits without biscuits!

Preheat your oven to 450°F and line a baking sheet with parchment paper.

In a large bowl, mix the flour, baking powder, and baking soda with the salt. Cut the butter into small pieces and toss it all into the dry ingredients. Using your fingers, quickly snap and rub in the butter until the pieces resemble baby peas. Make a well in the center of the dry ingredients, pour in 1¼ cups of the buttermilk, and give it a stir. The mixture should be quite sticky. If it's not, add another ¼ cup of buttermilk and mix just to combine. Turn the dough out onto a generously floured work surface and sprinkle the top with a little extra flour. Pat the dough down a bit, then fold it over onto itself. Pat it down again and fold it another four or five times, adding flour as needed, until you have a rough circle that's about 1 inch thick.

Using a 3-inch round cutter, punch out as many biscuits as possible, pressing straight down to get through the dough. Place the biscuits on the prepared baking sheet so that their edges almost touch. If you have any remaining dough you'd like to use, gather the scraps together and cut out some more biscuits. These ones might not rise as high as the others, but they'll be delicious all the same.

Place the biscuits in the freezer for about 5 to 10 minutes to firm up a bit, then brush the tops with melted butter and, if you're like me and love salt a little too much, give them a light sprinkling of kosher salt. Bake the biscuits for 14 to 18 minutes, or until they are tall, golden, and perfect.

Allow the biscuits to cool slightly and serve warm with lots of butter.

Outside the Box Brownies

MAKES 1 (9-INCH) SQUARE PAN

- ¾ cup unsalted butter
- 1½ cups granulated sugar
- 1 cup cocoa powder
- ½ teaspoon kosher salt
- 1½ teaspoons pure vanilla extract
- 2 eggs + 1 egg yolk
- ½ cup + 3 tablespoons all-purpose flour
- ½ teaspoon baking powder

I totally get why people love brownies. They're fudgy, dark, rich, and oh-so decadent. But, to be honest, I am one of those weirdos who only *really* likes brownies that come from a box. I know, I know, it's upsetting. But there is hope for me, and it is this recipe. I think I've finally figured out how to get those crispy edges, crackly top, and fudgy middle that is just the slightest bit cake-y. Once you've given these a go, you'll know what I'm talking about.

Preheat your oven to 325°F and grease and line with parchment paper a 9-inch square baking pan.

In a heatproof bowl placed over about 1 inch of lightly simmering water, combine the butter with the sugar, cocoa, and salt. Stir occasionally with a wooden spoon or heatproof spatula until everything has melted together and is warm to the touch, about 3 to 5 minutes. Remove the mixture from the heat and allow it to sit at room temperature for 5 minutes or so to cool slightly.

Stir in the vanilla and then the eggs, 1 at a time, followed by the yolk, stirring vigorously after each addition. Add in the flour and baking powder and stir for a strangely specific 40 to 50 times—this gets everything mixed up without producing too much gluten, so your brownies stay nice and fudgy. Transfer the brownie batter to your prepared pan and bake for 20 to 25 minutes, or until the top goes from shiny to a little matte.

Allow the brownies to cool in the pan and then serve.

Date Night

Aaron and I have a few restaurants that we absolutely love, but occasionally nothing beats a home-cooked feast. When I cook for Aaron, I love to make his favorites, which sometimes include meat. Even though I don't eat pork, beef, or poultry, nothing makes me happier than that big doofy grin he gets when he takes his first bite. The TV is off, phones are put away, and a record crackles away as we just revel in each other's company.

Grape and Rosemary Focaccia

MAKES ONE 9- X 13-INCH LOAF

- 2½ cups all-purpose flour, plus more for kneading
- 1½ teaspoons instant/rapid-rise yeast
- 1½ teaspoons granulated sugar
- 1½ teaspoons kosher salt
- ½ cup olive oil, divided
- ½ cup halved seedless red grapes
- 1 tablespoon finely chopped fresh rosemary leaves
- 1 teaspoon flaky or coarse salt

Sometimes nothing but freshly baked bread will do to satisfy my taste buds. Focaccia is a weekly project in my house, and with the addition of grapes and rosemary, this makes the perfect side for a date-night dinner table. Just be sure to serve it with oil, vinegar, and lots of red wine.

In a large bowl, combine the flour, yeast, sugar, and kosher salt and make a well in the center. Pour ¾ cup + 2 tablespoons of warm water into the well, along with ¼ cup of the oil, and begin mixing the dough with a wooden spoon. Once it's all combined, dump the shaggy dough onto a well-floured work surface and knead for about 6 to 8 minutes. Shape the kneaded dough into a smooth ball and place it in a well-oiled bowl. Cover the bowl with plastic wrap and a clean kitchen towel and allow the dough to rise in a warm place for 1 hour.

While it's rising, pour the remaining oil into a 9- × 13-inch baking pan, turning the pan to coat the bottom evenly, and set aside. Once the dough has risen, punch it down and press it into the oiled pan, making sure to poke your fingers all the way through to the bottom while you stretch the dough. Cover the formed focaccia with plastic wrap and a kitchen towel and allow it to rise in a warm place for 1 more hour.

Midway into the second rise, preheat your oven to 425°F. Once the dough has risen and is about double in size, scatter the grapes and rosemary over top and season with the flaky or coarse salt. Bake the focaccia for 15 to 20 minutes, or until golden brown and springy. Allow the bread to cool slightly and then serve warm or at room temperature.

Brisket and Mushroom Tagliatelle

SERVES 2 WITH LEFTOVERS

FOR THE BRISKET

1¼ lb brisket
½ teaspoon kosher salt
½ teaspoon freshly ground black pepper
2 teaspoons vegetable oil
1 small red onion, peeled and quartered
3 cloves garlic, smashed
2 carrots, peeled and cut into large chunks
3 sprigs thyme
2 sprigs rosemary
2 stems tarragon, leaves removed and reserved
2 cups dry red wine, such as cabernet sauvignon or montepulciano
4 cups no- or low-sodium beef broth
2 tablespoons ketchup
1 tablespoon liquid honey
1 tablespoon balsamic vinegar
2 teaspoons prepared horseradish

This is the perfect recipe for when you have a bit of time but don't want to put in too much effort. A little bit of prep, a quick trip to the oven, and some bubbling and sautéing will reward you with the richest and most delicious pasta this side of Tuscany. Even though I don't eat meat, the smell of this sauce as it cooks away for hours is enough to inspire the most romantic of feelings, making it ideal for date night.

Preheat your oven to 350°F and set a large Dutch oven over medium-high heat.

Cut the brisket into 2-inch cubes and season with the salt and pepper. Warm the oil in the Dutch oven and sear the brisket on all sides until deeply browned, about 1 to 2 minutes per side. Remove the brisket from the pot and add in the onions, garlic, carrots, thyme, rosemary, and tarragon stems. Lightly brown the vegetables in the pot for about 2 to 3 minutes, then deglaze with the red wine, scraping the bottom of the pot with a wooden spoon to release all of those browned bits. Add in the broth, ketchup, honey, balsamic, and horseradish, as well as the brisket and any juices that might have collected. Bring the mixture to a boil, cover, and transfer the pot to the oven to cook for 3½ hours.

When the brisket is super tender and cooked, transfer it to a bowl and strain the braising liquid through a fine mesh sieve, reserving all of the liquid. Pour the liquid back into the Dutch oven and, if you have more than 2½ cups of liquid remaining, bring it to a boil and reduce it to around 2½ cups.

Meanwhile, for the sauce, melt the butter and oil together in a sauté pan over medium heat. Sauté the garlic and shallots for about 1 minute, and then add in the mushrooms and season with salt and pepper. Cook until the mushrooms are golden, about 5 minutes, then set aside until the braising liquid has reduced. Once it has reduced, mix the corn-starch with 1 tablespoon of cool water and pour it into the reduced braising liquid. Continue to boil, stirring occasionally, until thickened, about 3 to 5 minutes. Stir in the whipping cream and turn down the heat to low to keep it warm.

FOR THE SAUCE

2 teaspoons unsalted butter
2 teaspoons extra virgin olive oil
2 cloves garlic, minced
1 shallot, minced
4–6 cups cleaned and chopped mushrooms, such as cremini, oyster, and Portobello
Kosher salt
Freshly ground black pepper
1 tablespoon cornstarch
¼ cup whipping (35%) cream
Reserved tarragon leaves

FOR SERVING

7–8 oz dry tagliatelle
Parmigiano-Reggiano shavings

When you're almost ready to serve, bring a pot of salted water to a boil and cook the tagliatelle until al dente. Shred the brisket with two forks and add it to the thickened sauce, along with the mushrooms. Allow everything to warm through and come together. At the last minute, stir in the tarragon leaves and serve over the tagliatelle with some Parmigiano-Reggiano shavings for garnish and deliciousness.

Note:

The brisket, sauce, and mushrooms can all be fully prepared a day ahead and stored separately. To serve, add in the shredded brisket and mushrooms to the sauce and reheat over medium-low heat while you cook the pasta.

TOP OF IMAGE: HERB SALAD (PAGE 228), FOCACCIA (PAGE 223)

BRISKET AND MUSHROOM TAGLIATELLE (PAGE 224)

Herb Salad with My Go-To Dressing

SERVES 2–3 (WITH LEFTOVER DRESSING)

¼ cup red wine vinegar
2 tablespoons smooth Dijon mustard
1 teaspoon grainy Dijon mustard
3 tablespoons minced shallot
1 teaspoon herbes de Provence
¼ teaspoon kosher salt
¼ teaspoon freshly ground black pepper
½ cup olive oil
4–5 cups lightly packed microgreens (see note)
½ cup picked flat-leaf parsley leaves
2 tablespoons fresh chives, cut into 1-inch pieces
A handful celery leaves, tarragon, basil, or any other fine herbs you might have lying around

I'm always amazed at how tasty a salad can be. Paired with my go-to dressing, the combination of fine herbs like tarragon, chives, basil, parsley, and celery leaves as well as teeny tender microgreens makes this seemingly unadorned salad a surprise standout on any table I bring it to.

In a large salad bowl, whisk the vinegar and both mustards with the shallots, herbes de Provence, salt, and pepper. Whisking constantly, drizzle in the oil and give the dressing one last good whisk to make sure the dressing is emulsified. Transfer the dressing to an airtight jar or container and set aside.

When you're just about to serve, toss the microgreens, parsley, chives, and whatever extra herbs you have lying around into a bowl and pour a few tablespoons of dressing over top. Give the salad a toss, adding more dressing if needed, and serve immediately.

Note:
If you can't find microgreens, arugula also works well.

Chocolate Almond Cherry Galette

SERVES 2 FOR A FEW DAYS OR 8–12 FOR DESSERT

FOR THE PASTRY

2 cups all-purpose flour
¼ cup cocoa powder
3 tablespoons granulated sugar
½ teaspoon kosher salt
¾ cup unsalted butter, straight from the fridge and cut into small pieces
⅓–½ cup ice-cold coffee (see note)
1 teaspoon pure almond extract

FOR THE FILLING

1 cup granulated sugar
¼ cup cornstarch
¼ teaspoon fine sea salt
3 cups frozen sweet cherries, thawed and liquid reserved
2 tablespoons lemon juice
1 teaspoon pure almond extract
¼ teaspoon freshly grated nutmeg

FOR THE TOPPING

1 egg + 2 teaspoons milk, for egg wash
¼ cup sliced almonds

Ice cream, for serving

There are few things more adorable and cringeworthy than the first stages of a new relationship. When Aaron and I met, we were pretty much babies. I was 19, he was 22. We were broke university students, so most of our dates consisted of walks in the park or sitting in one of our apartments, going through each other's music libraries. During one of these early walks, he proudly proclaimed that one of his greatest accomplishments in life had been winning the cherry pit spit competition in his hometown. To this day, I don't understand how one becomes proficient in this sport, or why it is a thing in the first place, but it was and continues to be pretty endearing. This dessert is always made with love for my guy, a true pie enthusiast and cherry pit spit champion.

For the pastry, in the bowl of a food processor fitted with the steel blade, pulse together the flour, cocoa, sugar, and salt. Add in the butter and pulse seven or eight times, or until the butter is broken up into hazelnut-sized pieces. In a small bowl, combine the cold coffee and almond extract and pour about ⅓ cup into the food processor. Pulse the dough another three or four times to incorporate. The dough should look like a bit of a mess at this point, but if you pick some up in your hand and squeeze, it should hold together. If it's still a little dry, add in the rest of the cold coffee and pulse to combine.

Place a piece of plastic wrap on your work surface and dump the dough on top. Wrap everything up and press it into a 1-inch-thick round. Refrigerate the dough for 20 to 30 minutes to allow the flour to hydrate and to re-chill the fat.

Meanwhile, make the filling by combining the sugar, cornstarch, and salt in a small pot. In a glass measuring cup, measure ⅔ cup of the juice from the thawed cherries. If there is not enough juice, just top it up with water to reach ⅔ cup. Add the juice to the sugar mixture and whisk to combine. Bring this mixture to a boil over medium heat and cook until thick, about 2 minutes. Remove from the heat, mix in the lemon juice, almond extract, and nutmeg and set aside to cool. When it's cool, fold in the cherries.

Preheat your oven to 375°F and line a baking sheet with parchment paper. Roll out the dough on a lightly floured work surface to a ¼-inch-thick circle. Transfer the dough to the baking sheet and top with the cooled cherry filling, leaving a 3-inch border all the way around. Fold the border up and over to form the galette. Brush the pastry with the egg wash and scatter the almonds over top.

Bake for 45 to 55 minutes, or until the crust is set. Allow the galette to cool slightly and then serve as is or with a big scoop of ice cream.

Note:

Pop a cup of coffee from your morning brew in the fridge to chill and use in this recipe.

It's Aaron's Birthday!

I am not a fan of my own birthday, but HOLY BANANAS do I ever love other people's days! This one is extra special because it celebrates another journey around the sun for my favorite guy.

Spicy Ginger Shandy

SERVES 2

- 2 (each 12 oz) bottles hoppy IPA
- 1 (12 oz) bottle non-alcoholic ginger beer
- 4 lime wedges

After being with my husband for about a decade, I've finally learned how to read him. When he *really* likes something, he's a quiet as a church mouse and with this drink in his hand . . . crickets.

Pour the bottles of beer into two pint glasses and split the ginger beer between them. Squeeze the juice from a lime wedge into each and garnish the edge with another wedge.

Berg's Burgs

SERVES 2 + 2 OTHER BIRTHDAY PARTIERS

- 2 tablespoons unsalted butter
- 2 small red onions, finely diced
- ½ teaspoon kosher salt
- ¼ cup pure maple syrup
- 1½ lb medium ground beef (see note)
- 1 egg
- 3 tablespoons dry bread crumbs
- 1 tablespoon finely chopped flat-leaf parsley
- 1 teaspoon finely chopped fresh thyme
- 1 teaspoon dried summer savory (see note)
- ½ teaspoon freshly ground black pepper
- 1 teaspoon smooth Dijon mustard
- 4 burger buns, toasted
- Dijon mustard, arugula, crispy bacon, mayo, and a mild, creamy blue cheese, to serve

A standard in our house all year long, these burgers are a necessity on Aaron's birthday. They are, after all, his all-time favorite food. In terms of toppings, I've listed Aaron's go-to choices but you can choose whatever your heart desires.

Melt the butter in a frying pan over medium-low heat and add in the onions. Season with the salt and cook until lightly caramelized, about 8 minutes. Add in the maple syrup and continue cooking until the onions are jammy and well caramelized, about 10 to 15 minutes. Remove from the heat and set aside to cool.

Meanwhile, in a large bowl, combine ¼ cup of the cooled maple caramelized onions, the beef, egg, bread crumbs, parsley, thyme, summer savory, pepper, and mustard. Using your hands, mix just until combined. Divide the beef into four evenly sized pieces and press into rounds about 1 inch thick. Sprinkle the outsides of the patties with more salt to season.

Preheat your grill or a skillet to medium/medium-high.

Cook the burgers to your desired doneness. I typically do 4 minutes on the first side and 3 minutes on the second, and then I top the burgers with cheese and cook them for an additional 1 to 2 minutes.

Allow the burgers to rest for 5 minutes before placing in the buns and dressing them with all of the fixings you can think of, including the rest of those maple caramelized onions.

Note:

For the tastiest burgers that can be cooked to any doneness, freshly ground beef from the butcher is the way to go. And if you can't find summer savory, add another teaspoon of finely chopped fresh thyme.

Zucchini Oven Fries

SERVES 4

- 1 tablespoon olive oil
- 2–3 medium zucchinis
- 2 tablespoons cornstarch
- 1 teaspoon kosher salt, divided
- ½ teaspoon garlic powder
- ¼ teaspoon cayenne pepper
- 2 eggs
- 1½ cups panko crumbs
- ¾ cup grated Parmigiano-Reggiano cheese
- ½ teaspoon freshly ground black pepper
- Cooking spray
- Mayonnaise or barbeque sauce, for dipping

For Aaron, the only thing that can make a burger better is a big side of french fries. While potatoes reign in my family, I've always found that perfect golden fries are tricky to recreate at home without the help of a deep fryer, so any time we are craving some crispy frites, these are a go-to.

Preheat your oven to 425°F and brush the olive oil in an even layer over a baking sheet.

Trim and discard the tops and bottoms of the zucchinis and cut each one into three. Cut each piece into small batons and set aside.

In a small bowl, combine the cornstarch, ½ teaspoon of the salt, the garlic powder, and cayenne pepper. In a separate shallow bowl or dish, beat the eggs. Finally, combine the remaining salt, the panko, Parmigiano-Reggiano, and pepper in a third dish.

Dredge the zucchini fries in the cornstarch mixture and then quickly dunk them in the eggs. Finally, coat them with the panko mix and place them in an even layer on your prepared baking sheet, leaving some space in between each one. Give the tops of the zucchini fries a good spritz of cooking spray and bake them for 30 minutes, giving them a turn after 20 minutes or so.

These are best served hot with a side of mayonnaise or barbeque sauce for dipping.

CLASSIC BIRTHDAY CAKE (PAGE 242)

Classic Birthday Cake with Too Many Sprinkles

MAKES 1 (5-INCH) FOUR-LAYER CAKE

3 egg whites
⅛ teaspoon cream of tartar
½ cup granulated sugar, divided
2 egg yolks
¾ teaspoon pure vanilla extract
3 tablespoons vegetable oil
¼ cup milk
¾ cup cake and pastry flour
¾ teaspoon baking powder
⅛ teaspoon fine sea salt
2½ tablespoons sprinkles
(see note, page 243)

There are certain things that demand a decadent stately cake, and a birthday is definitely one of them. This mini chiffon funfetti number is light, fluffy, colorful, and the most celebratory cake you could ever imagine. If you're looking to feed more than a few, double the recipe and you'll wind up with enough batter for an 8-inch three-layer cake. Bake the batter in three separate pans for the same amount of time listed for the mini version. As far as the buttercream goes, I'd double the recipe to make sure you have enough.

Preheat your oven to 325°F and line the bottom of two 5-inch spring-form pans with parchment paper. Be sure to leave the pans ungreased so that the chiffon batter can climb up the sides.

In the bowl of a stand mixer fitted with the whip attachment, whip the egg whites and cream of tartar until soft peaks hold, about 1 minute. With the mixer running, slowly sprinkle in ¼ cup of the sugar and continue to whip until the whites reach stiff peaks, about 1 to 2 minutes. Transfer the egg whites to a small bowl. Place the remaining sugar and the egg yolks in the bowl of your stand mixer. Using the whip attachment again, whip the sugar and yolks until light and almost doubled in volume, about 1 to 2 minutes. Add in the vanilla extract and, with the mixer running, slowly drizzle in the oil. Whip in the milk and sift in the flour, baking powder, and salt. Stir just until combined.

Remove the bowl from the mixer and, using a spatula, gently fold about one-third of the egg whites into the batter. Add the remaining egg whites and gently fold just until fully combined. Finally, fold in the sprinkles, being careful not to over mix.

Divide the batter evenly between the two prepared pans and bake for 30 minutes. Turn up the heat to 350°F and bake for another 10 to 15 minutes, or until the cake springs back when lightly pressed.

Leaving the cakes in their pans, invert them onto a wire rack so that they can cool upside down. This helps maintain the airy texture.

When they've cooled completely, run a sharp thin knife around the edges of each cake to loosen them from the pan. Release and remove the springform pan, level off the top of each cake, and slice each one into two layers. Then fill and decorate with the Swiss Meringue Buttercream (see below).

Classic Vanilla Swiss Meringue Buttercream

- 5 egg whites
- 1¼ cups granulated sugar
- ¼ teaspoon fine sea salt
- 1–1¼ cups unsalted butter
- ½–1 teaspoon pure vanilla extract
- Food coloring (optional)
- Sprinkles, for decorating

Note:
Use classic sprinkles (sometimes called jimmies) for this cake, as the small round variety tend to bleed their color into the batter.

Using a piece of paper towel, thoroughly wipe down the bowl of your stand mixer along with the whip attachment and a handheld whisk to make sure that they are all squeaky clean. Combine the egg whites, sugar, and salt in the bowl of your stand mixer and place it over a pot containing 1 inch of simmering water. Cook the whites, whisking frequently, for about 5 minutes until they show 150°F on a candy thermometer or until they are quite warm to the touch, the sugar has dissolved, and the mixture is no longer grainy.

Remove the bowl from the heat, return it to its stand, fit the whip attachment, and whip the cooked meringue on high speed until stiff peaks form and the bowl is cool to the touch, about 7 to 10 minutes. With the mixer running, add in about 1 tablespoon of butter at a time, allowing it to whip in a bit before adding the next tablespoon. Continue adding the butter until the frosting looks stiff.

There will be a point when adding the butter that the mixture will start to look like a mucky mess, but don't fret! It's called the curdle stage and it is totally supposed to look like that. It just means that you're almost done and a few more tablespoons of butter will bring everything together. When the buttercream is smooth and velvety, add in the vanilla and food coloring (if using) and whip to combine.

Use a piping bag fitted with a large round tip to fill the cakes. If you don't have a piping bag, you can use a large resealable plastic bag with the corner cut off. Swirl a full layer of frosting in between each cake layer. I do this by starting in the center and spiraling out toward the edge of the cake. To frost the outside of the cake, swirl a final layer on top, pierce a long skewer down through the middle of the cake to stabilize it, and pipe buttercream up the sides of the cake. Use an offset spatula, butter knife, or straight edge to carefully smooth the buttercream around the cake and then decorate with extra sprinkles and a few more dollops of buttercream. Don't feel like this needs to be perfect, either. The joy of a homemade birthday cake is that it looks homemade!

Menus from My Kitchen

In my house, every day is a kitchen party, so here are a few of my favorite menus to help inspire.

Bringing people together over a home-cooked meal is a tradition as old as any and I hope that I've been able to demystify the simple act of cooking and sharing. After all, from everyday dinners to grand celebrations, kitchen parties are all about delicious food, done as simply as possible, with as much love as you can muster.

Mother's Day for Mama B

Asparagus Zucchini Souffléd Omelet (page 24)

Leek Babka (page 36)

A pot of hot strong coffee

Backyard Picnic Brunch

Bourbon Sweet Tea (page 22)

Fried Chicken and Cornmeal Waffles with Spicy Maple Syrup (page 40)

Coconut Pecan Granola with Bourbon-Stewed Peaches (page 48)

Late Summer at the Cottage

Summery Corn Soup (page 105)

Bite-Sized Seafood Boil (page 116)

Roasted Napa Cabbage (page 138)

Berry Orange Slump (page 149)

Lots of ice-cold beer

Low-Key Bridal Shower

Marinated Olives (page 76)

Fennel, Citrus, and Burrata Salad (page 106)

Slow-Roasted Salmon with Tarragon-Chive Mayonnaise (page 126)

Raspberry Shortcakes with White Chocolate Lemon Curd (page 142)

Easter Switch-Up

Sweet Pea and Asparagus Soup with Lemony Crème Fraîche (page 108)

Pancetta Pork Tenderloin (page 122)

Squashed Potatoes with Gremolata and Feta (page 136)

Herb Salad with My Go-To Dressing (page 228)

Blueberry Upside-Down Lemon Cake (page 153)

Winter Revival

No-Knead Bread and Homemade Butter (page 102)

Brisket and Mushroom Tagliatelle (page 224)

Double Chocolate Almond Biscotti (page 146)

It's Thursday and Friends Are Coming Over

Maple Miso Spatchcocked Chickens (page 125)

Mashed Butternut Squash with Crispy Sage (page 199)

Pecorino Panko-Roasted Mushrooms (page 141)

Poppy Seed Almond Butter Palmiers (page 93)

Double-Date Night

Roasted Tomatoes (page 79)

Red Wine–Braised English-Cut Short Ribs (page 128)

Blue Cheese Polenta (page 132)

Maple-Glazed Parsnips (page 198)

Food Processor Flourless Chocolate Cake (page 145)

Thank You!

First and foremost, thank you to Myra, the one and only Mama B. If it weren't for your endearing ineptitudes in the kitchen and general hatred of making any sort of mess, I don't know if I would have ever found my haven by the hearth.

To Aaron, my perpetual taste-tester and the best roommate a girl could ask for, thank you for your undying support, love, high fives, and dish doing. Okay, bye-bye.

Extreme lasers of love and thanks to Michael for never being surprised when I accomplish something I never thought possible, to Marisa for pushing me toward this bananas new life, to Lindsay for constantly bursting into tears, and to Jenna for being my *real* taste-tester and lending your brilliant creative eye to this book and just my life in general. You leave everything you touch more beautiful than when you found it.

Fountains and fountains of thanks to each and every wonderful person who helped put this book together. To Robert McCullough, my publisher at Appetite by Random House, your passion for food and love of cooking is the *most* inspiring! It is now my life goal to have a room completely dedicated to cookbooks that I can Mary Tyler Moore twirl in whenever the whim strikes. Thank you for seeing something in *Kitchen Party* and for being a champion for this little lady and her book baby.

To the ladies of this project (Zoe, Jen, Lauren, and Jenna), you have all made every second of this experience complete magic. You are all wizards. Thank you for making this book look a zillion times better than I could have ever imagined!

Zoe Maslow, how did I ever get so lucky!? You are an editor extraordinaire and, other than the fact that you don't like cats, I think we are MFEO. You've made every second of this whole process an absolute dream, and I could not have done this without your constant encouragement.

Jen Griffiths, my own personal Gandalf! I truly cannot comprehend how someone can be so amazing at book design. Your work gives me goose bumps and I'm so honored to have had this book designed by you.

Lauren Vandenbrook, how in the world do you capture the feeling of a party so well and make food look so incredibly irresistible?! Working with you was an amazing, collaborative adventure and the fact that I got to share the making of *Kitchen Party* with family is oh-so-perfect. I think we nailed *gezellig*.

Gads of hugs and kisses to all those who sat around my table to taste recipes and listen to me yammer on about food and memories. A special thanks to Kyle, Marisa, Odie, Stock, Ross, Scott, Renee, Theo, and Paulie for bringing their gorgeous mugs to help out with the party shoots.

To Cathie James, thank you for seeing something in me and for making the introduction that got this whole delicious ball rolling.

Last but not least, thank you to you! Writing this book has been a true joy and a complete dream come true for me. While laboring over every single recipe in this collection, I grew more in love with each and every dish, and I hope that the recipes in *Kitchen Party* inspire you to open your home to those you love or, if you're more of a just-cook-for-my-family type, that they help inspire your daily meals.

Thank you for inviting me to your table!

Index